T0289858

PRAISE FOR
CYCLES

"I joined the FSC in 1972. Dewey's work inspired me to utilize cycles to fill in the blanks where traditional fundamental and technical analysis have no answer. Cycles have greatly benefited decision making during my investment career. I urge young investment professionals to study cycles now. Dewey's *Cycles* is the best starting point."

—**Bill Sarubbi, Cycles Research Investments**

"Since the 1970s, I have traveled the world teaching traders how to trade and investors how to invest. The perennial question that aspiring as well as veteran traders always ask is, 'Can you recommend a good book to help me learn how to become a better investor?' That has always been a difficult question to answer, but now that Dewey's book *Cycles* is available, that question has been answered.

If I had only had this incredible collection of research available to me when I first started trading in the late 1960s, I would have been even more successful and I would have avoided the 15 years of painful lessons I had to learn, in order to understand the markets. Dewey leaves no stone unturned in his research, his explanations, his theoretical considerations, and his examples. This incredible book is a must-read for any trader who has already been successful, or for those who want to improve their odds of success. I believe that if you are already making money trading, this book will help you make more. If you're not making money trading, this book will help you get on the winning track. No library of trading information would be complete without the Dewey book.

But be warned, this is not a 'get rich quick' book. It is a book that presents a theoretical construct of cyclicality, and then backs it up with hard evidence."

—Jake Bernstein, CEO, Network Press

"Kudos to Richard Smith and the newly energized Foundation for the Study of Cycles for bringing back into print Edward R. Dewey's classic book, *Cycles: The Mysterious Forces that Trigger Events*. Anyone interested in the rhythms of life on Earth should nurture an awareness of cyclic recurrences."

—Robert R. Prechter, *The Socionomic Theory of Finance*

"The study of cycles, like its subject matter, rises and falls in the public consciousness in lockstep with the ebb and flow of human affairs. Though a niche subject, some of the 19th and 20th century's most brilliant researchers devoted their time to it—Juglar, Kondratiev, Kitchin, Kuznets, Schumpeter and, of course, Dewey himself. It's astonishing to think that when he began his work in the 1930s the state of knowledge about things we take for granted now was so poor. For example, no one had a definite idea of how badly the Great Depression had damaged the American economy. Dewey's brilliant insights revealed so much of the underlying rhythms of our world and they are brought back to life in this important publication."

—Akhil Patel, *The Secret Wealth Advantage*

"If you have not read this classic book, you will never understand cycles. It is a must-have book."

—**Larry Williams, 61-Year Veteran Trader and Author**

"Edward Dewey was tasked in 1931 by President Herbert Hoover to seek out the cause of depressions. At the time, Dewey was Chief Economic Analyst for the Department of Commerce, and he found that depressions not only occurred rhythmically, they also happened regularly. In his opinion, 'cycles' could be used to anticipate periods of social unrest, predict stock market prices, forecast weather patterns, and project price fluctuations.

Cycles might not immediately be obvious, and their originating causes might be obscured, but every system is subject to them. They occur in the quantum arena of sub-atomic particles, and they occur in the orbits of the planets. What is less clear is that they occur in human activity. This presents a major problem for economic theory—especially where governments are involved.

Scientific endeavour is nevertheless approaching a major change in its understandings and, before too long, it will overtly recognise that what goes up must also come down. The idea of ubiquitous 'vibrations' is now attracting a great deal of attention. This book makes a good starting point."

—**Tony Plummer,** *Forecasting Financial Markets*

"Very few people realise the seminal importance of certain cycles. Edward Dewey was a pioneer in this field and his work stands the test of time. These patterns repeat not only in markets and economics, but also in nature and human behaviour. Understanding and implementation of this critical knowledge will provide you with a distinct advantage in life."

—**Andy Pancholi, Geopolitical and Market Strategist**

"Edward Dewey was my first study when I embarked on a lifelong mission to understand the market. I joined the FSC when I was 20 years old, and now find myself on its board! Now that I am older, my interest in cycles has never been stronger as I see them everywhere. Dewey has cemented a permanent place in history."

—**Brad Rotter, Financial Futures Pioneer**

"I am excited that the FSC and Harriman House are reintroducing the world to Dewey's world of cycles. My career began in earnest when I promoted a 212-week market cycle on Los Angeles television. It was due to resolve the week of December 9–13, 1974. On exactly December 9, 1974, one of the most important bottoms in market history was registered and I have Dewey to thank. The cycle was not his discovery but he was one of the main inspirations to me that led me to spend countless hours poring over market charts and seeking answers. Dewey presents a fascinating tale of his discovery of real-world cycles and his attempts to convince us all that they may well rule our lives. In a world that is constantly seeking 'reasons why,' I urge you to read this fascinating book. It helped to change my life. Could it change yours, too?"

—**Peter Eliades, StockMarket Cycles**

CYCLES

Every owner of a physical copy of this edition of

CYCLES

can download the eBook for free direct from us at
Harriman House, in a DRM-free format that can be read
on any eReader, tablet or smartphone.

Simply head to:

ebooks.harriman-house.com/cycles

to get your copy now.

CYCLES

The Mysterious Forces
That Trigger Events

Edward R. Dewey
with **Og Mandino**

HARRIMAN HOUSE LTD
3 Viceroy Court
Bedford Road
Petersfield
Hampshire
GU32 3LJ
GREAT BRITAIN
Tel: +44 (0)1730 233870

Email: enquiries@harriman-house.com
Website: harriman.house

First published 1971. This Harriman House edition published 2024.
Copyright © Foundation for the Study of Cycles

The right of Edward R. Dewey to be identified as the Author has been asserted in accordance with the Copyright, Design and Patents Act 1988.

Hardback ISBN: 978-0-85719-957-7
eBook ISBN: 978-0-85719-958-4

British Library Cataloguing in Publication Data
A CIP catalogue record for this book can be obtained from the British Library.

CONTENTS

Acknowledgments   xi

List of Figures   xiii

Foreword   xvii

1. The Mystery—and the Stage   1

2. The Search Begins   13

3. Nature's Mysterious Rhythms   25

4. Cycles in You   41

5. The Invisible Messenger   57

6. The Mob Cycles   71

7. The Rhythm of Production   93

8. The Cycle of Prices   113

9. The Cycles of Wall Street   131

10. Why Does it Rain on January 23?   159

11. The Patterns of War   175

12. Cycles in the Universe   189

13. The Ultimate Clue   217

14. The Imperative Question   233

ACKNOWLEDGMENTS

It is a pleasure to acknowledge the assistance of a multitude of people without whom this book could never have been written.

A grant of $500,000 from the W. Clement and Jessie V. Stone Foundation made possible not only the actual preparation of the book but also much of the research upon which the book is based.

Og Mandino—my alter ego—transformed a dull, ponderous volume that I had put together during the preceding three years into the sprightly, fascinating book that you are about to read.

All of the earlier research, and much of the later research upon which the book is based, was paid for by contributions from the members of the Foundation for the Study of Cycles. To them my everlasting gratitude, and to Gertrude Roessle, whose devoted service as manager of our membership department raised more than $1,000,000 for our research in the early days. (It is neither easy nor inexpensive to hew out a new science.)

Copley Amory, of Boston, our first chairman, was father to the Foundation and a second father to me.

My gratitude also goes to Chapin Hoskins, who introduced me to cycle study, and to the long list of cycle scientists from the biblical Joseph in the time of the Pharaohs to Great Britain's Lord Beveridge in the present century on whose shoulders I have stood, as others will on mine.

To my wife, Catherine, without whose patience in sacrificing herself to the cause by giving up evenings, Saturdays, and Sundays for over thirty-three years, my everlasting love and appreciation.

Specifically, I want to thank: Gertrude Shirk, who supervised the conduct of much of the research over a period of nearly twenty years; Dr. James Vaux, my successor as executive director of the Foundation, who has devised computer programs for our cycle analysis, thus condensing many days of work into a few minutes; Rosemary Chasey, who is responsible for the graphics; and all the other underpaid workers who over the years have helped to carry on the project.

Finally, I want to acknowledge the invaluable aid of Madeline Wilson, who as my assistant helped me prepare the original material on which this book is based, and Shane Rood, her successor, who has lightened my load and brightened my life for the past two years.

—E.R.D.
Pittsburgh, Pennsylvania

LIST OF FIGURES

1. Diagram of a Cycle
2. The 9.6-Year Cycle in Lynx Abundance, 1735–1969
3. The 9.6-Year Cycle in Atlantic Salmon Abundance, 1880–1956
4. Cycles in Brainwaves
5. A Grid for Recording Your Emotions
6. Lines of Force of a Bar Magnet
7. Mass Human Excitability, 500 B.C.–A.D. 1922
8. Presbyterian Church New Membership, 1826–1948
9. Congregational Church New Membership, 1861–1950
10. The Cycle of Guilt, 1923–54
11. The 18.2-Year Cycle in Marriage Rates in the United States, 1869–1951
12. The 8.9-Year Cycle in Death Rates in Massachusetts, 1865–1961
13. The 18.2-Year Cycle of Immigration into the United States, 1824–1950
14. Annual Cycles of Crime (after Hoover)
15. Is This a Clue to Our Mystery?
16. The 6-Year Cycle in General Electric Orders Received, 1896–1946
17. The 5½-Year Cycle in Airplane Traffic, 1930–55
18. The 6.4-Year Rhythm in Aluminum Production, 1885–1962
19. The 18⅓-Year Cycle in Real Estate Activity, 1795–1958
20. The 8-Year Cycle in Cigarette Production, 1879–1958
21. The 6-Year Cycle in Steel Production, 1874–1947

22. The 33-Month Cycle in Residential Building Construction, 1920–55
23. The 9.6-Year Cycle in Wheat Acreage Harvested, 1868–1947
24. The 9-Year Cycle in Life Insurance Sales, 1858–1962
25. The 9.18-Month Cycle in Ton-Miles, Canadian Pacific Railway, 1903–48
26. Benner's 9-Year Cycle in Pig Iron Prices, 1834–1900
27. The 54-Year Cycle in European Wheat Prices, 1513–1856
28. The 3½-Year Cycle in Corn Prices, 1860–1948
29. The 17¾-Year Cycle in Cotton Prices, 1740–1945
30. The 16⅔-Year Cycle in English Wrought Iron Prices, 1288–1908
31. The 17¾-Year Cycle in Pig Iron Prices, 1872–1950
32. The Price of Oats, 1950–59
33. A Stock Market Forecast
34. Trends and Cycles
35. Three Cycles and Their Combination
36. The Individuality of Stocks
37. The 9.2-Year Cycle in Stock Prices, 1830–1966
38. The 41-Month Rhythm in Stock Prices, 1868–1945
39. The 41-Month Rhythm, upside-down, 1946–57
40. The 7.6-Year Cycle in New York's Barometric Pressure, 1874–1967
41. The 4.33-Year Cycle in Philadelphia's Precipitation, 1820–1960
42. The 4.33-Year Cycle in Baltimore's Precipitation, 1820–1960
43. Wheeler's Phases in Climate
44. Earthquakes and Sunspots, 1829–96
45. The 142-Year Cycle in International Battles, 1050–1915
46. The 57-Year Cycle in International Battles, 1765–1930
47. The 22⅕-Year Cycle in International Battles, 1415–1930
48. The 11⅕-Year Cycle in International Battles, 1760–1947
49. The War Cycles, combined, 1930–70
50. Index of International Battles, 1820–1958

51. Electromagnetic Wave Spectrum
52. Average Annual Sunspot Numbers, 1700–1968
53. Sunspots and Terrestrial Magnetism, 1835–1930
54. Sunspots and Manufacturing, 1875–1931
55. The Double Sunspot Cycle, 1700–1968
56. Abbot's Cycle of St. Louis Precipitation, 1860–87
57. Various Other Weather Cycles, 1934–39
58. Solar Radiation at Calama, Chile, April 1920
59. A Cycle in a Variable Star, 1922–30
60. A Cycle in a Quasar
61. Planetary Relationships
62. The 5.91-Year Cycles on Parade
63. The 8-Year Cycles on Parade
64. The 9.2-Year Cycles on Parade
65. The 9.6-Year Cycles on Parade
66. The 18.2-Year Cycles on Parade

FOREWORD BY DR. RICHARD SMITH

I T'S VERY GRATIFYING to bring this important work back into print in collaboration with Harriman House. The study of cycles and their influence on our individual and collective lives is enjoying a renaissance through the works of Neil Howe, Ray Dalio, Howard Marks and others. We welcome this opportunity for others to learn about this seminal work.

Edward R. Dewey was a pioneer in the study of cycles. His work in this area dates back to 1929 when he was hired by the Department of Commerce. He quickly became the Chief Economic Analyst for President Hoover, where, as Dewey put it, "Talk about being where the action is. Let me tell you, *I was there!*"

Dewey was tasked by President Hoover to figure out why depressions happened. "I was assigned the task of discovering why a prosperous and growing nation had been reduced to a frightened mass of humanity selling apples on street corners and waiting in line for bowls of watery soup."

He gradually lost faith in the ability of economists to answer his question because every economist he spoke with seemed to have a different explanation. He became convinced that something was missing from the study of economics and he eventually concluded that this was a knowledge of cycles. He wasn't the only one.

When Dewey established the Foundation for the Study of Cycles

(FSC) in 1941 he was joined by leaders from the Smithsonian, Yale, Columbia, Harvard, the Institute for Advanced Study at Princeton, and several major corporations, as well as leaders from Canada and Great Britain. Moreover, the Foundation was truly an interdisciplinary undertaking, spanning economics, astronomy, biology and geology.

First published in 1971, *Cycles: The Mysterious Forces That Trigger Events* was written at the pinnacle of Dewey's 40-year quest to develop a "new science of cycles." It is a record, as he says, "of our successes, our failures, our hopes, our doubts, our frustrations, and our progress." Let's take a brief look at one of the cycles he studied extensively.

THE 41-MONTH CYCLE IN U.S. STOCK PRICES

One of the cycles documented by Dewey, and the one that will likely intrigue many new readers today, is a 41-month cycle in U.S. stock index prices from 1868–1957, as highlighted in Chapter 9.

Using the cycle detection methods developed by Dewey and others at the FSC, a similar analysis from the early 1950s to today reveals that a 41-month cycle (though a few weeks longer than the one Dewey identified) has indeed persisted through to the present day.

The solid black line in the accompanying chart is a detrended history of weekly data on the S&P 500. The dashed zig-zag line is an idealized 41-month cycle (182 weeks, to be precise). While the correspondence between the actual and idealized tops and bottoms isn't perfect, there clearly remains a remarkable 41-month pulse in U.S. stocks. Moreover, it has been particularly evident since the 2008 top.

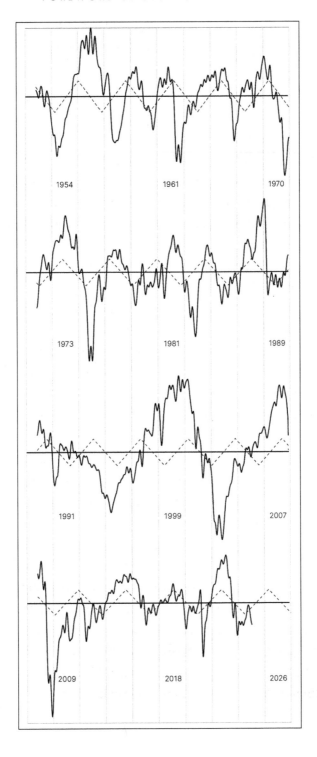

THE PRESENT AND THE FUTURE
OF THE STUDY OF CYCLES

Were Dewey still with us today, he would surely be both thrilled and a bit disappointed with the progress made in the study of cycles since his death 45 years ago.

On the one hand, he would be astounded with the technological progress since his day, especially in the areas of computational capacities and data collection. One of my personal joys at being involved with the FSC today is going through the archives, which are full of Dewey's careful and beautiful handwritten efforts to collect data and identify cycles without the aid of computers. Documenting and discovering cycles was clearly a labor of love for Dewey. He would be in awe of our modern capabilities.

He would also be delighted with the renewed recognition that the study of cycles is receiving today through the work of prominent authors like Neil Howe (*The Fourth Turning*), Ray Dalio (*Big Debt Cycles* and *The Changing World Order*), Howard Marks (*Mastering the Market Cycle*), Peter Turchin (*End Times*), and George Friedman (*The Storm Before the Calm*).

On the other hand, Dewey would be a bit disappointed that these efforts and advances are taking place in relative isolation from one another, and that little effort is being made to advance an interdisciplinary science of cycles.

Dewey was clear that, for him, "comparative cycle study is the name of the game." He said, "We *compare* cycles in all phenomena, searching for similarities and possible relationships among them." He was interested, for example, in why there were observable 9.2-year cycles in phenomena as disparate as common stock prices, tree rings, lake levels, and grasshopper abundance.

Dewey's burning question was, "Are there unknown environmental forces, predictable in their effects, that influence human beings and other forms of life and even nonlife here on earth—and, if so, what are they and how do they operate?"

Dewey's question remains a powerful—yet controversial and challenging—question for us today. As Dewey himself observes early on in this classic work that you are about to explore, the notion that we are all "pulled this way and that by environmental forces" is "unsettling" and "demeaning to our self-esteem."

Neil Howe similarly observes, in *The Fourth Turning Is Here*, that the idea of cycles "would strip those of us who live in the modern world of our most treasured privilege—a free and open-ended future in which we can aspire to be different from or better than our ancestors."[1]

The study of cycles has long been looked upon in the West as a questionable approach for understanding how our world works and what the future might hold. Whether it be Augustine in the Fourth Century warning against "invalidating salvation" by believing that "the sky is responsible for your sin," or our modern obsession with precision, specialization and the march of progress, a systematic and scientific study of cycles has not yet gotten the full attention it deserves.

It should not be a shocking hypothesis that there may be "tides in the affairs of men," of which we remain unaware. Indeed, it would be more shocking if there were no such tides given how prominent rhythmic patterns are in our world.

Dewey hoped and believed that a knowledge of cycles would yield fruits such as the end of war and disease and the accurate prediction of weather a year or more in advance. While we may be more tempered from our own vantage point over half a century later, we should keep in mind that the first half of the twentieth century was a heady time for science and technology.

---

1   N. Howe, *The Fourth Turning Is Here* (Simon & Schuster, 2023), p. 30.

He was also honest about the fact that he could not yet explain the origins of the cycles he collected and catalogued. He saw his own work as being more akin to that of an early field biologist—collecting samples and analyzing data and sharing his work with other researchers and the public. He called others to the study of cycles.

It is often in periods of crisis that we find a renewed interest in the study of cycles. People begin to look beyond the ideals of linear progress as they search for deeper explanations for why things don't seem to be going quite so well as they once were. That was certainly true in the early days of Dewey's research and it is true again today. Why dig deeper, after all, when a rising tide is lifting all boats?

My own belief is that a recognition and appreciation of the unceasing and inescapable influence of cycles in our lives can help us to better regulate the highs and the lows. It can help us to remember during the upswings that the good times will not go on forever and, during the downturns, that better days lie ahead.

It's when we fail to discover and acknowledge the influence of cycles that we really get ourselves into trouble. Neil Howe compellingly makes this point when he points out that, "The society that believes in cycles the least, America, has fallen into the grip of the most portentous cycle in the history of mankind."[2]

Edward Dewey saw the same thing over 80 years ago. His pioneering work and leadership in the study of cycles deserves wider recognition and we welcome the renewed interest that this new edition of his classic book will bring.

More importantly, we welcome the renewed interest in the study of cycles. Far from being merely a fearful study of the

---

2 *The Fourth Turning Is Here*, p. 35.

chains that bind us, a proper study of and respect for cycles opens paths of enhanced productivity, progress and peace as we learn to recognize and to cooperate with the many beautiful cycles of our treasured world.

—Dr. Richard Smith

Executive Chairman, Foundation for the Study of Cycles

"By the Law of Periodical Repetition, everything which has happened once must happen again and again and again—and not capriciously, but at regular periods, and each thing in its own period, not another's, and each obeying its own law... the same Nature which delights in periodical repetition in the skies is the Nature which orders the affairs of the earth. Let us not underrate the value of that hint."

—Mark Twain

1

The Mystery— and the Stage

FOR OVER A million years man has been trying to predict his future.

He has always failed—and his failures are buried in the dust of history. Legendary fortune tellers, prophets, oracles, medicine men, astrologers, numerologists, mystics, charlatans, and seers, all claimed possession of supernatural and occult powers that enabled them to see into the future. Wars were fought, kingdoms fell, and civilizations were altered as a result of their pronouncements and predictions.

We are not without their counterparts today. They invade our homes through the media of television, radio, and the press, claiming hidden and mysterious powers that enable them to solve murders, foretell earthquakes, and blueprint our days in advance. They play on latent superstitions within all of us, piously predicting the next political assassination, the next airline tragedy, the next Hollywood divorce.

But, working quietly behind the scenes, thousands of scientists in fields as unrelated as history, botany, anthropology, mammalogy, terrestrial magnetism, sociology, and economics—to name only a few—are accumulating facts and figures that promise to make this age-old dream of foretelling the future at least a partial reality. A new science which deals with the behavior of events recurring at reasonably regular intervals throughout the universe may ultimately enable us to predict, scientifically and accurately, the events of tomorrow.

The consequences and responsibilities represented by this embryonic science are almost too staggering to comprehend. Try to imagine a world where we will know, in advance, the probabilities of when the next war will begin, when the next civil unrest will erupt into a riot, when the next panic will descend on the stock market, when the next flu epidemic will strike, and when the next great flood or earthquake will occur.

And what of lesser events? How would the Parisian salons operate if all of us could forecast what the fashions for milady will be next year? How would Detroit's automakers react if they could accurately forecast that our choice in automobile colors for the next model year will lean toward a variety of blues instead of this year's popular greens? Would moviemakers abandon pornography and turn to musical comedies if it could be predicted that the latter will be our preference eighteen months hence?

We are just beginning to probe one of nature's basic secrets— rhythmic repetitions of events. And when we unlock the last door to our quest we will have the answer to what may well be the greatest mystery in the world—cycles, and their cause.

WHAT IS A CYCLE?

Place your hand on the left side of your chest.

Feel your heart beat? You are feeling a rhythmic cycle—something that occurs again and again at a more or less uniform time interval, a rhythm.

Our world contains hundreds of similar cycles, occurrences that repeat with predictable regularity. Tides ebb and flow every 12½ hours. There is the twenty-four-hour alternation of day and night. The moon reappears every twenty-five hours. Woman experiences a twenty-eight-day menstrual cycle. The seasons come and go on schedule. All these cycles, and countless more, are understandable and explainable. There is no mystery.

But there are thousands of rhythmic cycles in our world for which there is no logical explanation, *no known cause*. At present we know little more about cycles than was known about chemistry in the days of Boyle, Cavendish, Priestley, and Lavoisier, the fathers of modern chemistry, who made their pioneering discoveries only a brief 175 years ago. We know little more about cycles than was known about germs before Antonie van Leeuwenhoek, in 1675, looked through his famous microscope at a drop of rainwater and saw his first microbe. Until that marvelous day no living man had seen these little wriggling creatures. No man knew that *there was a whole subvisible world existing under his very fingernails*!

There is much in common between the new world discovered by Leeuwenhoek and the new world discovered by early cycle pioneers. In 1838, Dr. Hyde Clarke, of England, was the first to notice rhythmic ups and downs (cycles) in business activity; Ernest Thompson Seton, the American naturalist, was one of the first to call the public's attention to the rhythmic variation in the population of animals; and Samuel Benner, in 1875, was the first American to recognize rhythmic cycles in prices.

These men, and many others, noticed regularities caused by

something, they knew not what. But they glimpsed a hint of forces abroad in the universe—forces surrounding us and influencing us—that had hitherto been as unknown as Leeuwenhoek's bacteria. Their discoveries opened up a whole new world in which to adventure. When these forces and their laws have been removed from the realm of the unknown it should be possible to throw light on the coming of epidemics, on future weather conditions, on the future abundance of wildlife, and on hundreds of other natural mysteries.

But far more important, if these unknown forces affect the behavior of human beings as they seem to, we find ourselves at the very core of the problem of wars and depressions. For if wars and depressions are not caused by generals, businessmen, or politicians, as the mass of the people believe, but are the results of—or at least are triggered by—natural physical forces in our environment, we are on the threshold of a completely different and extraordinary way of life for all mankind.

THE WORLD OF CYCLES

The science of cycles deals with events that recur with reasonable regularity. Such events may be in nature, business, or anything else. The important thing about regularity is that it implies predictability. And if you know an event is coming, you can often prevent it or avoid it if you wish. Or if you cannot prevent or avoid it, you can at least prepare for it so that its effect on your life is lessened.

Most people do not realize the extent to which cycles and regularities exist in the world. Here are only a few examples:

Atlantic salmon vary in abundance in a cycle that averages 9.6 years from peak to peak. Starting with the year with the heaviest salmon population, the fishing gradually gets worse and worse for four or five years. Then the fish start to increase in numbers. Fishing improves each year for four to five years, so that eight to ten years from your starting point the fishing is excellent again. These years of good fishing have come at intervals averaging 9.6 years apart for as far back as there are records.

In Illinois chinch bugs vary in population in a cycle that averages 9.6 years.

The abundance of snowshoe rabbits in Canada varies in a cycle of the same 9.6 years. So does the population of lynx, marten, fishers, owls, and hawks.

Heart disease in the northeastern United States has been found to fluctuate in a cycle of the same duration. The acreage of wheat harvested in the United States varies according to the same cycle.

After this, it would probably not surprise you to learn that grasshopper outbreaks and mouse plagues come in cycles that have a duration of 9.6 years. But they don't. Grasshopper plagues come 9.2 years apart. Mouse plagues come four years apart—in Presidential election years. Why?

Pine cones are more plentiful in cycles. People join churches in cycles. Prices of every commodity so far studied rise and fall in cycles. Women are more amorous in cycles. Sunspots erupt in greater numbers in cycles. Poets are more creative in cycles. The weather fluctuates in cycles, and so do the fashions in clothes. Why?

The consumption of cheese fluctuates in cycles. The number of international battles fluctuates in cycles. The number of earthquakes fluctuates in cycles. Real estate activities fluctuate in cycles, as do the prices of common stocks. Why?

Male emotions fluctuate in cycles, as do industrial accidents. The sales of every company so far studied fluctuate in cycles, as does the incidence of many diseases. Why?

Cancer recurs in cycles, glaciers melt in cycles, and the levels of lakes and rivers rise and fall in cycles. Advertising effectiveness fluctuates in cycles, as do human intellectual activity and the cattle population. Even political landslides and the number of infants born per day fluctuate in cycles. Why?

In many instances the regular rhythm is undoubtedly the result of chance. But are *all* these cycles, some of them recurring time after time for hundreds of years, merely chance phenomena? Can we arbitrarily blame them all on chance when we discover that many of them, in phenomena completely unrelated to each other, have their highs and lows *at the same time*—as if their rhythms were all being controlled by a single gigantic metronome?

SOMEWHERE OUT THERE

Many cycles in nature seem to have the same wavelength as cycles in human affairs, and some cycles found on earth seem to have the same wavelength as cycles found on the sun. The other planets may even be involved, and the implications are strong that the solution to the mystery of the cause of cycles will be discovered somewhere in the universe—"somewhere out there."

The dimensions of the stage on which this search will take place are awesome. Stand anywhere on the earth and you will be able to see approximately 2,500 stars on a clear night. Imagine for a moment that each star, actually a flaming ball like our sun, has been transformed into a grain of rice. If this were so, you could hold all 2,500 visible stars in a single hand.

But there are over 100 billion stars in our galaxy alone—and if every star were only a grain of rice you would need more than forty railroad cars to hold them all! And our galaxy is only one of 100 million galaxies, each rotating slowly in a cycle of its own, each following its own path in the universe.

Just as grains of rice help us to visualize the star population, let us borrow a few fruits and vegetables to reduce heavenly distances to a scale we can understand. We will begin with one large pea, a quarter-inch in diameter, as our earth. A small seed, one quarter as big, placed only nine inches away, is our moon. Using this scale of dimensions, our sun would be a giant melon, about thirty inches in diameter, almost the length of a football field away. Mercury and Venus would be peas spinning around the sun between the sun and earth. Now 423 feet from our sun let us place another pea, Mars. Then we walk a quarter of a mile and drop an orange, Jupiter. We travel another quarter of a mile and place down another orange, Saturn. A mile from our sun we drop a plum, Uranus; Neptune, another plum, is dropped at a mile and a half; Pluto, a pea, at two miles.

Merely to lay out our own solar system (remember, the size of our earth on this scale is a pea) would require a field four miles square. Then, of course, to make things complete you would have to add dust to represent the 1,500 asteroids, the comets (more than a thousand of them), and various moons, each with their cycles of rotation and revolution.

Now the true immensity of our task is upon us, for in order to position accurately the nearest star to earth we must leave our four-mile-square field and travel 14,000 miles! To continue until we have covered *only the stars in our own galaxy* on the same scale we must travel 3½ times the real distance to our sun!

And yet evidence is mounting that there is "something out there"—some force, or forces, that affect every living thing on earth, and it does so with rhythms that have taken man through cycles of war and peace, prosperity and depression, optimism and despair, discovery and isolation, morality and degradation, creativity and ignorance, famine and plenty.

TIME: THE YARDSTICK

While you are still trying to relate the size of your own neighborhood to the vastness of space, let us consider time and age.

In all cases we measure the recurrence of cycles by time—fractions of a second, seconds, minutes, hours, days, weeks, months, years, centuries, millenniums.

CYCLES: THE MYSTERIOUS FORCES THAT TRIGGER EVENTS

Some electromagnetic waves have cycles so swift that they are measured in billionths of a second. The sun, on the other hand, makes its circuit of our galaxy in a cycle of 230 million years.

At the turn of the century many people actually believed that the world was created in 4004 B.C. Today the generally accepted age of our universe is approximately 15 billion years. Our earth, however, is a youngster, only about 5 billion years old.

Do you know how long 5 billion years is?

Let's try to comprehend this planet's age through another simple scale with proportions we can all understand. An effective method that I used years ago when teaching was to load my students in my car and say, "Now we are going to take a twenty mile drive to such-and-such a monument. We will let this twenty-miles represent the time from the creation of the earth to the present. As we go along I will point out when various things happened—such as the solidifying of the earth's crust, the beginning of life, the emergence of the earliest mammals, the appearance of the earliest men, the beginning of recorded history, when the United States was born, etc."

On our scale of twenty miles to 5 billion years it was quite surprising to the students how many miles we had to drive before we came to the first life on earth—some sixteen miles, if I remember correctly. Man, however, did not appear until forty feet from the end of our journey. Recorded history began only *one inch* prior to "now"; and the United States appeared only in the last *1/20th of an inch*!

Peas, plums, oranges, rice, melons—and a twenty-mile ride in the country. Did they help you, in some small way, to comprehend the grandeur of That Which created and sustains the universe—call it God or Nature or whatever you prefer?

MAN'S GREAT MENTAL CHANGE

What you have been able to grasp in the last few moments required thousands of years for our predecessors to understand. Revising our estimate of the time of the earth's creation from 6,000 years ago to 5 billion years ago—from 1½ inches to twenty miles—is perhaps the greatest revision in knowledge in human history.

This mental change also applies to our concepts of mass and space. Three hundred years ago people thought that our little planet was the whole universe except for a couple of lanterns hung in the sky by God to give us light by day and by night, and a handful of fireflies scattered up there for no particular reason. Since then man's "universe" has changed, first from the conception of our planet to our solar system, then from our solar system to our galaxy, then from our galaxy to the entire universe.

The widening of our mental horizons has been accompanied by revolutionary changes in knowledge and technology that are even more startling. Twenty-five years ago all that was known about steroid chemistry could be contained in one slim notebook. Today all four walls of a large room, floor to ceiling, are required to hold the books and papers recording our knowledge in this field.

In our grandfathers' time ($1/50^{th}$ of an inch ago on our twenty-mile scale) it required six weeks or more for a letter to travel from New York to San Francisco. Now we can watch athletes competing in the Olympic Games halfway around the world as the events are happening. A little over $1/100^{th}$ of an inch ago we were earthbound. Today we not only soar in the air faster than any bird but we have broken our bond with the earth and its gravity, confidently looking toward a future of interplanetary space travel.

Further examples are superfluous. The point, I think, has been made. The present—the last $1/100^{th}$ of an inch—is the most exciting and wonderful time to live in of all the ages since the beginning of the world.

IS MAN ONLY A PUPPET ON A STRING?

Yet as man brushes away his cobwebs of ignorance, as man acquires new knowledge of himself and his universe, he is swiftly approaching a point in time when he will be confronted with what may be a basic secret of nature, for the evidence is mounting that we are surrounded by cyclic forces, of which, as yet, we know almost nothing. These forces bounce us like marionettes on a string. They make us fight; they make us love. And all the while we think we are doing these things solely for rational reasons.

This is an unsettling concept. It ranks with the discovery that the earth is not the center of the universe, that man is not a special creature but has roots in the animal kingdom from which he developed, or that many of man's actions result from subconscious loves and hates of which he is ordinarily ignorant.

Since it is demeaning to his self-esteem, it is perfectly understandable that man should resist any hypothesis that holds that his life and his universe vibrate in rhythms that are regular and at least partially predictable and are caused by a force or forces still unknown and possibly uncontrollable by him.

Nevertheless, the evidence that man is not one step down from the angels, sublimely in command of himself and his world, continues to accumulate. He is more like a character in a Punch and Judy show, pulled this way and that by environmental forces. And he will continue to be so manipulated until he solves the mystery of these forces. Only then will he be able to cut the strings and become himself.

"*Ignorance lies at the bottom of all human knowledge, and the deeper we penetrate the nearer we come to it—for what do we truly know, or what can we clearly affirm of any one of those important things upon which all our reasonings must of necessity be built, time and space, life and death, matter and mind.*"

—Charles Caleb Colton

2

The Search Begins

I N SEPTEMBER OF 1929, just a few weeks before the world we knew disappeared in miles of ticker tape and crashing stock prices, I was hired by the Department of Commerce as Chief of Industrial Marketing. Later I became the Chief of Current Statistics too. Finally I was promoted to Chief Economic Analyst. Talk about being where the action is. Let me tell you, *I was there!*

In 1931, as a heartbroken President Hoover watched the country he loved falling apart before his eyes, I was assigned the task of discovering why a prosperous and growing nation had been reduced to a frightened mass of humanity selling apples on street corners and waiting in line for bowls of watery soup. Why did depressions happen? As liaison officer with economists both inside and outside the government, it was my task to find the answers.

I consulted many economists—and nearly everyone had a different theory to explain our economic sickness. It was almost as if you were ill and one doctor said you had gout, the next said you had cancer, a third diagnosed your trouble as leprosy, and a fourth said you had athlete's foot! If doctors disagreed about illnesses in this way, you would not have much faith in doctors. Economists disagreeing as radically as they did, I lost faith in economists, for none of them knew the answer.

CYCLES ENTER MY LIFE

Then one day I met a man who *knew* he didn't know the answer. His name was Chapin Hoskins, the Managing Editor of *Forbes*. He too had despaired of learning from economists why depressions happen. But he reasoned logically that if he couldn't discover "why," perhaps he could at least learn "how." He began to study the *behavior* of prices, production, and other measures of economic activity.

In the course of his studies Hoskins noticed that every three months there was a slight upsurge in the bank debits of certain cities. In these cities, every three months, checks totaling larger amounts were drawn. He had discovered a cycle!

Before we proceed, let me be sure you understand the word. "Cycle" comes from a Greek word for "circle." Actually, the word cycle means "coming around again to the place of beginning." It does not, by itself, imply that there is a regular period of time before it returns to the place where it started. When there is such a fairly regular period of time, the correct word to use is "rhythm," from another Greek word meaning "measured time." As we mentioned, the tides are rhythmic; your heartbeat is rhythmic; so is your breathing. A cycle, when we refer to one, will usually mean a cycle with rhythm (see Figure 1).

Fig. 1: Diagram of a Cycle

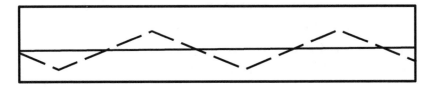

A cycle comes back to the place where it started. A rhythmic cycle comes back at reasonably regular time intervals.

Getting back to our friend Hoskins: He didn't know "why" bank debits had this three-month cycle. He didn't need to know why. Every three months it happened. It was worth taking into account as a probability in trying to assess the future.

Presently Hoskins observed that in some instances every third one of his three-month upsurges in bank debits was larger. He had discovered a nine-month cycle. Some things had this nine-month cycle without having the three-month cycle. His interest increased when he discovered that there were even longer cycles. The most important of these seemed to be about forty-one months in length. This pattern was so regular and had repeated itself so many times that it did not seem to him to be the result of chance. His study of behavior was becoming even more fruitful than he had dreamed, for he had discovered the possibility of predicting when things would be high, when they would turn downward, when they would be low, and when they would turn upward again!

Hoskins accumulated a great quantity of data. Then he began to make forecasts based on his observances. These forecasts came true. The possibility had become an actuality! Here, indeed, was something of importance.

In those days, even as now, you could find hundreds of individuals willing to help you select "hot" stocks, tell you how the stock market would act next month, and even read tomorrow's

Dow Jones closing averages in tea leaves—all for a fee, of course. Men of good sense laughed at them then, just as they do now.

But no one laughed at Chapin Hoskins, for this genius, a member of the Board of Directors of the American Management Association, had impeccable credentials. Westinghouse Electric's Executive Vice President was also a member of the board. He followed closely the forecasts made by his brother board member, and finally he engaged Hoskins on a two-year retainer to teach Westinghouse all that he knew about cycles. Furthermore, he assigned his chief designing engineer to Hoskins and hired two professors from Cornell to review the Hoskins techniques. Something was finally being done about cycles.

In 1937, on the strength of his contract with Westinghouse, Hoskins started up in business as an analyst for industrial companies. I joined him as an associate. My job was to go out and sell firms on the benefits we could provide by helping them to forecast their future sales, production, cost of raw materials, etc., through the application of the cycle theory. I would sell the accounts; Hoskins would do the forecasting. The arrangement reminded me of the story of the hod carrier. The hod carrier said that he had a fine job; all he had to do was to carry bricks up six stories and the man up there did all the work.

Chapin Hoskins and I started in business on March 1, 1937. I'll never forget our first day together. I had just purchased a few shares of stock and mentioned it to Hoskins along with my hope that I would reap great profits when the stock went higher.

"It won't go any higher," he said. "Sell everything you have at once. We are within a week of the top. If I had just a little more courage, I'd go short with everything I've got."

Sure enough, within a week the market did reach a top and the disastrous decline of 1937–38 had begun.

Later that year, in August, the market started upward again. I was in the office of a famous investment counselor, a man who handled millions of dollars for his clients. I heard him tell one of them, "The decline is over. Buy heavily." I knew from what Hoskins had taught me about cycles that the worst part of the decline was still ahead. I tried to convince the counselor of this but he wouldn't listen. I've often wondered if he didn't later wish he had! From August 1937 to April 1938 the Dow Jones Industrials fell from 184 to 113, a decline of 39 percent.

Chapin Hoskins and I succeeded. Eventually we had more business than Hoskins could handle. Our clients included such large companies as Botany Worsted, Consolidated Edison, and Lehman Brothers. Soon I began to do some of the research, counseling, and forecasting, and my interest in cycles reached a new height. I began to spend more and more time at the libraries, reading everything I could find on the subject.

THE MEETING AT MATAMEK

One memorable library visit set my future course irrevocably on the trail of the great cycle mystery. I came across a transcript by Professor Ellsworth Huntington of Yale University of a conference that had been held in 1931 in Matamek, Quebec, on the north shore of the Gulf of St. Lawrence.

About the time when I had been anxiously interviewing economists to discover the cause of our Great Depression, a Boston financier named Copley Amory had organized an international conference on biological cycles that was held at his summer estate in Matamek. Twenty-five of the world's leading biologists assembled to compare notes about cycles in wildlife. As I read the transcript of their findings, a strange excitement took hold of me, for I learned a fact known to every sportsman, namely, that game is sometimes plentiful and sometimes scarce. But what impressed me was that the periods of abundance, and of scarcity, often came at amazingly regular time intervals. Cycles!

THE SEARCH PARTY IS FORMED

I discovered something else on that fateful day when the transcript of the Matamek Conference came to my attention. I learned of the cycle work that had been done by C. N. Anderson of the Bell Telephone Laboratories. Anderson had discovered that sunspots act as if they were influenced by a variety of cyclic forces similar to those that Hoskins and I had been discovering in business figures and also to those that the biologists had discussed at Matamek. Cycles in business! Cycles in wildlife! Cycles on the sun! And, in many instances, these cycles *had the same length and went up and down together.* Now here was something basic, something fundamental, something more profound than I could envision. For if two or ten or a hundred separate and seemingly unrelated things fluctuated in cycles of identical wavelength and turned at about the same time, it was unlikely that they were as unrelated as might first be supposed. Either some of them were causing the others to behave that way, or *something hitherto unknown and unsuspected* was causing all of them to go up and down together. Do you see the mystery, the excitement? A detective story on a cosmic scale!

I saw at once that we were confronted with a basic scientific problem that could be solved only by linking together economics, biology, and astronomy—and perhaps several other sciences as well. The problem had to be attacked on a broad front.

I set to work at once. On October 23, 1940, I organized the Foundation for the Study of Cycles. I wrote to Copley Amory, the chairman of the committee of biologists, and to Ellsworth Huntington. Mr. Amory came to see me and was as surprised to learn about the economic and astronomical cycles as I had been to learn about the biological ones. He agreed that the problem needed to be attacked as a whole. He approved of the idea of a Foundation for the Study of Cycles and agreed to become chairman of our board of directors.

Mr. Amory and I then reorganized the permanent committee set up at Matamek; its members were elected as the board of directors of the Foundation.[3]

Mr. Amory presented the Foundation with a check for $500, and we were afloat. I was "hired" as the director, and it has been my privilege, with the help of our members, to keep the Foundation afloat for the past thirty years. The Foundation for the Study of Cycles is now affiliated with the University of Pittsburgh, and its headquarters are located at 124 South Highland Avenue, Pittsburgh, Pennsylvania. In this book you will learn of our successes, our failures, our hopes, our doubts, our frustrations, and our progress.

PUTTING THE PIECES TOGETHER

Suppose that one day while digging in your back yard you came across some bits of stone that were so regularly shaped that they could not easily have been formed that way by chance. Suppose, further, that some of these pieces fitted together as if forming part of a larger pattern.

You would be quite excited, wouldn't you? "I have stumbled across some magnificent old mosaic," you might say.

Every evening, weather permitting, you would be in your yard, digging and screening dirt. You would bring all the little stones

---

3   The original board of directors consisted of the following persons:
UNITED STATES OF AMERICA: Charles Greeley Abbot (Secretary, Smithsonian Institution); George Baekeland (Bakelite Corporation); Hon. William Cameron Forbes (Chairman of the Board of Trustees, Carnegie Institution of Washington); Hon. Alanson Bigelow Houghton (Chairman, Corning Glass Works & Chairman, Institute for Advanced Study, Princeton University); Ellsworth Huntington (Professor of Geography and Climatology, Yale University); Wesley Clair Mitchell (Director, National Bureau of Economic Research & Professor of Economics, Columbia University); Harlow Shapley (Director of the Observatory, Harvard University); and Copley Amory (Chairman of the Foundation).
CANADA: Hon. Charles Camsell (Commissioner of the Northwest Territories, Canadian Government); Frank Cyril James (Principal and Vice Chancellor, McGill University).
GREAT BRITAIN: Hon. Patrick Ashley Cooper (Governor, Hudson's Bay Company); Charles Sutherland Elton (Director, Bureau of Animal Population, Oxford University); Julian Sorrell Huxley (Secretary, Zoological Society of London).

into the house, scrub off the dirt, and rinse them carefully. Some pieces you would discard because they were obviously just stones; some pieces would unquestionably be part of the mosaic; others you might not be sure about.

The good pieces and the pieces you could not be sure about you would save. You would put them on a table and you would try to fit them together wherever you could. Some you would place to one side since they would not fit any of the pieces you already had. Soon a pattern would begin to take shape. You would become more and more excited. "What a stupendous discovery!" you would say. "I am really on the track of something big!"

So it is with the study of cycles. We dig them up, scrub them, rinse them, shine them, and put them on the table. Some are so regular that there seems to be no question that they are significant. With others we cannot be so sure. Some fit together with other pieces. Some do not fit at all. And, most exasperating of all, some almost fit—but not quite.

It is impossible to count how many pieces of the cycles mosaic we have found to date. In 1946, when *Life* magazine was planning an article on cycles, their editors asked me to give them a list of all the rhythms I had ever heard about. Although the list I eventually sent them was neither complete nor authoritative (and contained many rhythms that were controversial or unsubstantiated), I managed to itemize 308.

Eighteen years later the Foundation published a catalog listing only the alleged cycles in economics—commodity prices, stock prices, agriculture, building construction, real estate, manufacturing, etc. The catalog contains 1,280 cycles.

Because small keys can unlock great doors, we at the Foundation have treated every hint of a possible cycle with great respect and deference. No "stone" we uncover is tossed aside as irrelevant, for we believe we are assembling far more than a mosaic.

THE FIVE CATHEDRALS

You may remember the story of the two stonemasons. When asked what they were doing, the first said, "I am surfacing a piece of stone." The second answered, "I am building a cathedral."

Although it has "surfaced" many stones since its birth in 1940, the Foundation for the Study of Cycles believes it is building a cathedral—several of them, in fact.

CATHEDRAL NUMBER ONE:
The Advancement of Human Knowledge

We are doing our part toward learning how the universe functions, for we are discovering evidence of hitherto unsuspected forces. Learning how the universe functions is, to my mind, the noblest activity of the human race. It is, literally, reading the word of God.

CATHEDRAL NUMBER TWO:
The Elimination of War

There is little hope of eliminating war for yourself, your children, or your grandchildren. But—hopefully—you will have great-grandchildren. It is for them we are building.

Wars come in cycles. That is, the number of international battles tends to pulsate at reasonably regular time intervals. Wars act as if they were stimulated by regularly recurring cyclic forces.

These forces are presumably external to human life, for even when the rhythm of war is disturbed, it returns to the old pattern. And the rhythms are much the same as those we find in animal life and other aspects of nature.

As part of the problem of eliminating war we must understand these rhythmic forces and how they operate. But even before we do, it is of great benefit to know when the next international "situation" can probably be expected.

CATHEDRAL NUMBER THREE:
The Elimination of Depressions

Only by understanding the forces that cause depressions can we ever learn to control them. There is a growing mass of evidence that depressions recur at rhythmic time intervals. So far as they have been studied, all the various aspects of depressions—curtailed production, business failures, unemployment, financial collapse— act as if they are influenced by rhythmic forces, the nature of which is still unknown. Until we learn what these forces are and how they operate any true science of economics is impossible. But until we solve this mystery our limited knowledge of cycles can help throw some light on *probable* future economic fluctuations of a disastrous nature.

CATHEDRAL NUMBER FOUR:
The Elimination of Disease

As yet only a small amount of cycle research has been done in this area, so the importance of cycle knowledge in the elimination of disease has not been determined. However, anyone who has suffered from the flu bug in the last few years may be interested to learn that there is evidence that even this little monster visits us in cycles—in spite of the development of "wonder" drugs.

CATHEDRAL NUMBER FIVE:
Accurate Weather Forecasting
a Year or More in Advance

How wonderful it would be if farmers could know in advance when to expect droughts, late frosts, or rainy harvests. What savings in seed and heartache there would be.

Our foresters would also rejoice in such foreknowledge. So would our mariners, our hydroelectric companies, our flood control experts, our military leaders—even our football, baseball, and racing fans.

Other fields could be named, for there are *thirty-six different aspects of science* where a knowledge of cycles is important. The Foundation's main purpose is to bring together the stones and rocks from all these various fields and raise an altar to the glory of God… and to the benefit of his children.

"We cannot impose our wills on nature unless we first ascertain what her will is. Working without regard to law brings nothing but failure; working with law enables us to do what seemed at first impossible."

—Ralph Tyler Flewelling

3

Nature's Mysterious Rhythms

ONE EVENING IN 1940, I gave a talk, illustrated with slides, to the New York chapter of the American Statistical Association. After the meeting I happened to overhear one professor say to another, "I never saw so many coincidences in my life!"

What that scholarly gentleman meant, of course, was that the cycles I had illustrated and discussed were nothing but coincidences. I might have agreed with him about any one cycle, but I had faith that all of them could not possibly be coincidences. At that time, however, this was merely faith on my part, and I knew it. That faith has been strong enough to nourish me for more than three decades, and it has grown stronger with the years as I have watched "coincidence" piled on "coincidence," as the pieces began to fit together, and as the clues to the mystery were uncovered in mounting numbers. Faith is now being justified by indisputable fact.

I have never been one to go off the deep end by confusing *thinking* and *feeling* with *knowing*. "It looks as if there is something here,"

I would say to myself as I studied a series of figures, "but of course it may be nothing but chance, nothing but coincidence." (In the early days we did not know how to determine, mathematically, the number of times out of 100, or 1,000, or 10,000 that any particular cycle could come about by chance.)

How can one tell, in any given instance, whether or not a regular rhythm that one discovers is caused by a real underlying force or merely by chance? Let's begin with some common sense and simple logic. If a cycle has repeated *enough* times, with *enough* regularity, and with *enough* strength, the chances are that it is significant. Such regularity cannot reasonably be mere accident.

Pick up a pack of playing cards and begin to deal, face up. The first card is red, the second black, the third red, and the fourth black. You now have two waves of a regular cycle—red, black, red, black. This could easily happen by chance.

You continue to deal. Red, black, red, black. Four times in a row now. This regular alternation could still be chance, but it couldn't be chance if it were to continue much longer.

Resume dealing. Red, black, red, black, red, black. Seven times now! It could still be chance but it is less and less likely. It begins to look as if somebody has stacked the cards. You go through the entire deck. Twenty-six times of alternating red and black cards! "Somebody certainly stacked this deck," you exclaim. "It couldn't happen this way by chance once in a million times."

You underestimate! The mathematical odds that black and red cards would alternate in twenty-six waves, accidentally, are *one in a quadrillion*! In this chapter you will be introduced to cycles that have repeated at least twenty-six times over a period of more than two hundred years. Later on you will meet cycles that have repeated more than one hundred times—*back to the year 600 B.C.*!

WILL NATURE'S CLUES
SOLVE OUR MYSTERY?

In the past thirty years a considerable amount of our research at the Foundation has involved cycles in the natural sciences, for three important reasons. First, rhythmic cycles are almost universal in nature. Second, natural science cycles are usually much less complicated than human cycles and thus easier to study. Third, when the wavelengths of natural science cycles are the same as wavelengths of cycles in the social sciences we have reason to believe that we are approaching the very heart of our mystery.

Unless you have studied the subject, you would be amazed at the universality of rhythmic cycles in nature. The abundance of birds, fish, insects, reptiles, microorganisms, and mammals fluctuates in rhythm. Tree rings, evidence of annual growth, are wide and narrow in rhythmic cycles. Water levels in our rivers and lakes go up and down in cycles. Earthquakes recur at rhythmic intervals. So do volcanic eruptions. Sedimentary rock deposits are first thick and then thin in layers that evidence rhythm. All aspects of weather show rhythmic cycles—although very complicated ones—and, of course, many stars pulsate rhythmically.

Thus we study rhythms wherever they can be found, not because we have any special interest in ornithology, herpetology, ichthyology, or geology, but because the cycles in these and other branches of natural science are often identical with the cycles of man. Because they are identical *they may have a common cause*.

For example, there is nothing very remarkable in the fact that there is a similar eight-year cycle in stock prices and in manufacturing production. You might expect that the one would go up and down with the other. However, if the weather *and* earthquakes *and* sunspot eruptions *also* have eight-year coincident cycles, you are confronted with a situation that makes you feel you are on to something big.

Studying nature's behavior, then, may teach us more about man's behavior. So, like Alice in *Through the Looking Glass*, we will momentarily turn our back on what we wish to know so that we will know it better. We will face in the other direction, away from the social sciences, and review a few mysterious cycles in wildlife, something that the United States Army Air Force, to their regret, once neglected to do in the early months of World War II.

THE BATTLE OF ASCENSION ISLAND

Ascension Island is little more than a few square miles of volcanic matter situated in the Atlantic Ocean halfway between South America and Africa. It was selected in 1942 as an ideal spot for the Army Air Force to build a stopover landing field for their short-range medium bombers, which were unable to cross the ocean nonstop. Hurriedly they built their field, and the B-25's and the B-26's began their endless procession across the Atlantic. Ascension Island, however, is accustomed to another type of winged visitor, for it is the nesting ground of the sooty tern, a bird with a unique breeding cycle. It returns to its favorite breeding ground every 9.7 months to hatch its oversized eggs!

But the Air Force was not aware of this rhythm of nature, and soon after the landing strip was completed, thousands upon thousands of terns began swarming over the field, which, unfortunately, had been built in the middle of a nesting area.

The small web-footed creatures were more than a nuisance; they were a frightening hazard to the fliers. Whenever a plane took off or landed, the startled terns would leave the ground and fill the sky with tens of thousands of pounds of flying gull meat only slightly less dangerous than antiaircraft shells. Although the Air Force, in order to save lives and planes, might have been tempted to consider "genocide" on the sooty terns, they could not, for they had promised to respect the flora and fauna of the island.

To help resolve the dilemma, Dr. James P. Chapin, an ornithologist with the American Museum of Natural History, was consulted. Eventually he collected sufficient data to compute that terns returned to nest every 9.7 months on the average. After discarding several ideas to force the birds to move away, he finally hit upon the simple process of breaking their eggs. He had learned that the parent bird rarely returned to the scene of a nesting that had ended in disaster. By forcing the adult birds to move elsewhere, he not only saved them as future breeding stock, but undoubtedly saved the lives of many young pilots.

What brings the sooty tern back in a 9.7-month cycle? In more temperate climates of the world, which have wide variations of climate, temperature, and weather conditions, birds have an annual breeding cycle. But Ascension Island is near the equator. There is no distinct change in the weather from season to season, nor is there any variation in the amount of daylight. Yet every 9.7 months a million or more terns arrive at Ascension to hatch their young.

THE ODD-YEAR BIRD

A small North American bird with the unlikely name of evening grosbeak is another winged creature with a baffling cycle. It migrates into New England in large numbers—but only in the odd-numbered years. Only three times since 1913 have the grosbeaks deviated from their strange timetable. They were due in 1915 but failed to show, coming instead a year later. In 1917 they returned to schedule, but came again in 1918 also. In 1937 they never bothered to show up at all. Except in these years they have made their appearance every odd-numbered year with dramatic regularity.

That the grosbeak's regularity was not perfect, over the years, demonstrates an important characteristic of many cycles: after an interruption they tend to return to their old rhythm. In 1937, when it was due, the grosbeak did not appear, but it did not come the next year either. It waited until its next "due" year, 1939, to return. The reason for this invasion of New England in an almost perfectly regular two-year cycle is not yet known.

THE STAY-AT-HOME BIRD

Nearly all bird populations fluctuate in cycles. Studies by J. Murray Speirs of the Research Council of Ontario concentrated on birds that frequent the Toronto region. He discovered that the northern shrike, the rough-legged hawk, and the snowy owl have populations that fluctuate in cycles of three to five years. The pine grosbeak has a five-to-six-year cycle, and the horned owl has a cycle of nine to eleven years.

Dr. Leonard W. Wing, through another study, concluded that the hairy woodpecker, the downy woodpecker, and the bobwhite have an abundance cycle of 50.7 months. Changes in bird abundance are usually associated with their migrations. Many experts feel that food scarcity, which seems to occur at cyclic intervals, forces birds to move toward strange but warmer country. Eventually, when their search is rewarded with a surplus of food, their fertility increases, they multiply, and they spread out over larger land areas.

But the bobwhite's activities almost destroy this explanation, for few of these small reddish-brown birds ever die *more than a mile* from the nest where they were hatched. Migration cannot possibly affect their population fluctuations, and yet they have a definite cycle of 50.7 months. Whatever force causes this cycle does so in their own neighborhood. And this force is not yet known.

THE RISE AND FALL OF THE LYNX

The Canadian lynx is another prime example of one of the most baffling aspects of animal life: its rise and fall in population—the cycle of abundance. Patrolling the northernmost regions of Canada in search of his favorite food, the snowshoe rabbit, the lynx moves with huge running strides on padded feet large enough to prevent him from sinking into the soft snow. But while he is a hunter, he is also the hunted, for his skin is instantly convertible to cash at the nearest trading post.

Unless we are trappers, hunters, or fishermen, we normally think of animal populations as relatively stable, a notion that is far from actuality. Animal populations vary tremendously from year to year, even from month to month. Since the lynx is a favorite of north-country trappers, year-by-year records of its population are available over a long period of time, and it thus makes excellent study material.

Of course, there are no actual lynx censuses, but there are records of the offerings of lynx skins by trappers, particularly to the Hudson's Bay Company. As the efforts of trappers to earn a livelihood are fairly constant, biologists feel that the records of skin offerings constitute a reasonably reliable index of the abundance of the animal in its wild state.

Now I ask you to look at an almost unbelievable "picture" of a cycle (see Figure 2). Note that this 9.6-year cycle in Canadian lynx abundance has been repeating itself in almost perfect rhythm since 1735.

Fig. 2: The 9.6-Year Cycle in Lynx Abundance, 1735–1969

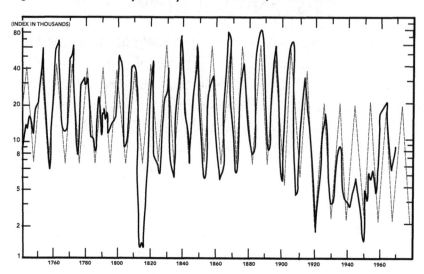

Note: To help you visualize the regularity of the cycle under discussion a broken zigzag line diagramming a perfectly regular cycle of the same length will be included in all cycle charts.

Except for the fact that during the last fifty to sixty years the catch has been considerably lower, the most notable features of this record are the tremendous fluctuations that characterize these figures and the amazing regularity of the fluctuations. The graph shows a range from under 2,000 skins in a poor year to over 70,000 in a good one. Intervals between one high and the next, or one low and the next, normally vary from eight to ten years. Over the span of the record they average precisely 9.6 years.

Because of the wide fluctuation in skins from a high year to a low, and because of its regularity, the Canadian lynx cycle has received wide attention. Although there is general agreement that it has not continued to fluctuate in such a regular rhythm for over two hundred years purely by chance, there is little agreement as to the cause.

One attempted explanation is based on a similar cycle in the rise and fall of abundance of snowshoe rabbits, the most important item of food in the lynx diet. But this raises an obvious and unanswered question. What causes the 9.6-year cycle in the snowshoe rabbit?

The 9.6-year cycle in population is characteristic of much wildlife. The coyote, red fox, fisher, marten, wolf, mink, and skunk have abundance cycles of the same period (average wavelength), all reaching their highs and lows in abundance at about the same time on the calendar.

In Illinois, and in much of the Midwest, a pesky white-winged insect called the chinch bug also has a 9.6-year cycle, at the peak of which up to 70 million have been known to cover one acre, wreaking havoc on cereal crops. Since it is rather difficult to imagine 70 million of anything, this reduces to 1,600 bugs per square foot!

SALMON, LOST AND FOUND

Atlantic salmon fluctuate in abundance in a cycle whose period is identical with the lynx in Canada and the chinch bug in Illinois (see Figure 3).

Fig. 3: The 9.6-Year Cycle in Atlantic Salmon Abundance, 1880–1956

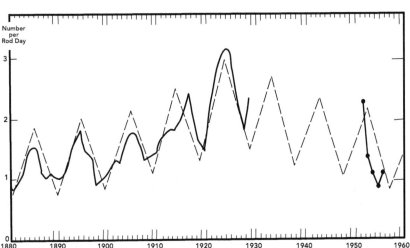

Restigouche Salmon Club catch per rod per day, smoothed, 1880–1929; values 1952–56 actual. No other values available.

The Restigouche Salmon Club is an ultraexclusive group of sportsmen who fish for salmon on the Restigouche, a river approximately 125 miles long flowing between the Gaspé Peninsula and New Brunswick and emptying into the Gulf of St. Lawrence. Careful records kept by its members of the catch of salmon per rod per day indicate that the abundance of salmon fluctuated in a 9.6-year cycle from 1880 to 1930. More recent figures supplied to me by the club's president pick up the identical rhythm, which is in step with the previous cycle. This is an important piece of evidence, indicating that here is a cycle that cannot possibly be ascribed to chance. I will elaborate on the significance of this in a later chapter.

In another 1960 study, traces of the same 9.6-year cycle in Atlantic salmon were discovered thousands of miles away in Wye, England.

The practical use to which cycle knowledge can be put is obvious in our brief look at salmon abundance, for the problem of occasional scarcity in this popular seafood is of vital importance to the European fishing industry. To be able to predict the good and bad years for salmon fishing can save thousands of man-hours and millions of dollars. We need not wait until we solve our mystery to take advantage of knowledge we already possess.

THE RODENT WHO DIES IN A CYCLE

The Norwegian word for "destroying" is *lemmus*, or lemming. On the average of every 3.86 years a six-inch rodent by the same name sweeps down from the hills of Norway in hordes, destroys everything in its path, and continues on until it reaches the sea. But it doesn't stop at the water's edge. It continues on, destroying itself by drowning. A few, who for some inexplicable reason remain behind, become the nucleus for the new horde that will migrate

3. NATURE'S MYSTERIOUS RHYTHMS

toward the sea, on the average, 3.86 years later. The cause of the lemming's rush to death on such a regular schedule is not known.

Norway also has a 3.86-year cycle in the abundance of foxes, and in the United States the growth of limber pine seems to have an identical cycle length. What obscure force could possibly affect the growth of certain trees in America and also influence the lemmings and foxes of Norway?

TREES, PRICES, AND ELECTRICITY

In the last paragraph I mentioned tree growth. Measuring this growth is accomplished simply by measuring the varying widths of tree rings. Trees grow by adding layers of wood. Winter growth is hard and compact. Summer growth is soft and porous. Cut down a tree and you can measure its rings for the growth of any particular year. When the tree has had a good year of growth, the layers for that year are thick; when growing conditions are poor, the layers are thin. There is a tendency for several pairs of thick layers to be followed by several pairs of thin layers. When this alternation is regular, we have rhythmic cycles in the tree ring widths.

Arizona trees and their rings have been the subject of study for many years. One study, which traced the growth of trees back to the ninth century, indicates a fifty-four-year cycle. In England, coal, pig iron, and lead production have the same cycle length. France has a fifty-four-year cycle in imports and exports and total foreign trade. In 1922, Lord Beveridge noted a fifty-four-year cycle in wheat prices, and the United States is now old enough to have experienced three such cycles in average wholesale prices. Coincidences?

Other cycles of a shorter length have also been discovered in tree rings, and one in Arizona of 16⅔ years has also been discovered in the trees on Java.

A third tree ring cycle, forty-two years in length, is of interest because it has characteristics that we find in many of our cycle studies. Its forty-two-year cycle repeats for perhaps ten regular waves and then we will have only one high in the next eighty years or so. Then we might have two waves where there should be three. Finally it resumes its old and regular forty-two-year rhythm as if the force that caused the forty-two-year cycle always existed but was diverted, for a time, either according to chance or to some law not yet understood.

Trees have another fascinating cycle. Their electric potential, or voltage, goes up and down in rhythm. If you drill two small holes vertically, a yard or so apart, in the trunk of a living tree and insert one end of a piece of wire into each hole, an electric current will flow along the wire, as if the tree were an electric battery. With a battery, however, the voltage is constant. In a tree the voltage varies. Also, the current from a battery always flows one way, but the current from a tree sometimes flows one way and sometimes the other.

Dr. H. S. Burr of Yale University has kept constant records of changes in voltage for a number of trees in the New Haven area, day and night, for many years. His records disclose two startling facts. First, the voltage in trees goes up and down in a cycle of approximately six months. Second, another tree of the same kind, even thirty miles away, behaves in the same manner. When the current flows up in one tree, it does the same in the other. When it flows down in one, it does likewise in the other. Dr. Burr attempted to link this change in voltage to possible similar changes in the barometric pressure, temperature, or humidity in the area, but eventually he abandoned all of these as the possible cause for the trees' strange behavior.

Let us examine this "clue" for a moment. What could possibly cause trees to act this way? Obviously the cause must be environmental. Something *unknown* in the air or in the earth must influence their behavior. But what? Since we see the effects we know there must be a cause. Something does exist to make trees act this way and this "something" has force, a force that repeats in a cycle. What is this force?

THE CLEARINGHOUSE

In their search to understand nature, several generations of scientists have noted the existence of rhythmic behavior. Working in their own field of interest, they often observed and commented on what seemed to be patterns and subpatterns in events. But prior to the creation of the Foundation for the Study of Cycles there was no clearinghouse that could gather information about cycles in meteorology, let us say, and pass this on to those doing research with cycles in economics, medicine, agriculture, or sociology. Some scientists, even today, are not aware of cycles in any field but their own.

Yet if cycles are truly characteristic of all living things, is it not logical that a knowledge of cycles, in animal abundance, for example, might provide the geologist or the meteorologist with information that could reinforce his own discoveries? Without this valuable interchange of cycle information between the various branches of science, will these dedicated people ever truly understand their own particular science?

Although your only interest in bugs may be to destroy those who feed on your rose bushes, let's assume for the moment that you are an entomologist and your life's work has been the study of the grasshopper. Because of your research you are aware that crop losses and pest control expenses caused by these insects deprive farmers of millions of dollars each year.

However, your studies have been long and thorough and you are aware of the fact that the population of grasshoppers fluctuates in cycles and hence is partially predictable. You know that there are at least three cycles in the abundance of grasshoppers, one with a period of 9.2 years, one with a period of 15 years, and one with a period of 22.7 years. It is as if several forces were influencing their abundance simultaneously.

Now, of course, all three of these cycles are meaningful in your work but you are particularly interested in the 9.2-year cycle because it is the shortest one, and thus repeats most often. One day you happen upon some of the material published by the Foundation for the Study of Cycles, and what you read dumbfounds you, for you learn that the same 9.2-year cycle exists in many other phenomena. There are cycles of similar length in the water level of Lake Michigan, in the alternate thickness of tree rings, in business failures, and in prices. A 9.2-year cycle has been continuously present in pig iron and copper prices since 1784; a 9.2-year cycle has been evident in industrial stock prices since their beginning in 1871, in railroad stock prices since their beginning in 1831. Partridge abundance in Hertfordshire, England, shows a cycle of approximately 9.2 years, and tree rings at Santa Catalina, Arizona, tend to be thicker at 9.2-year intervals.

Later you discover other "coincidences." From an old issue of *Cycles*, the Foundation's monthly magazine, you learn that the Smithsonian Institution has published a paper by Dr. C. G. Abbot, based on forty years of observations, that states that radiation of heat from the sun varies in cycles of approximately 22.7 years, the same length as your longest grasshopper cycle. Also, in the same issue, you encounter your long cycle again at, of all places, an old Bohemian estate in Krumau, Czechoslovakia. Data on the annual bag of partridge from this estate covering a period from 1727 to 1909 show highs and lows at 22.7-year intervals.

The odds are great that your work in entomology will never be quite the same again. You will realize for the first time that the cycles you are dealing with in grasshoppers may be part of something much larger, and of fundamental importance to the world.

THE LOWEST FORM OF LIFE

No book that you can comfortably hold could catalogue all the known cycles in natural science. There are endless numbers of rhythms, some lesser known, such as the cyclic hatching of many insects, cyclic pigment changes, cyclic metabolic rates, cyclic chemical changes of the body—even cyclic variation of milk produced by cows. There is also the rhythm of feeding patterns of many animals, including bedbugs, chipmunks, rabbits, and lizards.

Even the amount of pollen gathered by bees fluctuates in a cycle.

Unlike Noah, I have made no attempt to include every species in my "ark," for it would sink from sheer weight and you would eventually cease reading from boredom. The purpose of this chapter has been accomplished if you are now aware that there is rhythm in nature. Later on you will meet many more cycles in nature as we compare them to cycles in other sciences.

But before we leave the birds and the bees and the lynx and the salmon there is one more cycle in nature that I cannot resist introducing to you. Drifting in the oceans and many freshwater lakes of the world are microscopic organisms called plankton. Although plankton is one of the lowest forms of life, it is, nevertheless, an important source of nourishment for most of the creatures that inhabit the underwater world.

Lowly though it may be, it has one thing in common with the grasshopper, the salmon, the partridge, the lynx, and even the tree. *It has a cycle of its own.* In 1926, a study of plankton in Lake Michigan was initiated by the Water Purification Division of Chicago, and by 1942 more than 12,000 samples had been taken from the lake. The average annual total plankton yield suggested the occurrence of a periodic four-year cycle in which two rather high production years are followed by two rather low production years.

As with many of the tiny plankton's larger brothers and sisters in the world of nature there is no logical or accepted explanation for this cycle.

"Summer follows winter, new moon follows old, day follows night... The universe is not static; every component from an electron to a galaxy is continually moving and such movement cannot proceed forever in the same direction. Sooner or later it must complete a circle, or stop and return in the opposite direction."

—J. L. Cloudsley-Thompson

4

Cycles in You

NATURE AND ALL its components fluctuate in cycles. Her greatest creation, your body, is no exception.

You breathe, and your lungs expand and contract in rhythm. Your heart and pulse join in the anatomical parade— but their cadence is different from that of your lungs. Your blood pressure and blood flow are also cyclical, as are your adrenal secretions, your bile production, and your body temperature.

Even your brain operates in a rhythmic way (see Figure 4), producing wavelike electrical impulses that range from one wave every few seconds to very rapid impulses of thirty or more per second, an important factor in medical diagnosis of various diseases.

Fig. 4: Cycles in Brainwaves

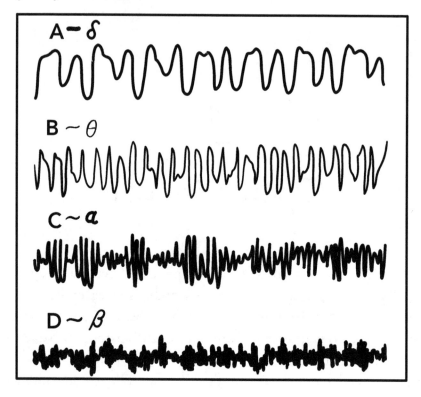

The four main types of brainwaves (after Walter).

Amazingly the bacteria in your body have a cycle of abundance—just like the lynx, the salmon, and the partridge.

YOUR DAILY RHYTHMS

You live on a tiny wet ball in space, a sphere rotating on its axis in a twenty-four-hour period relative to the sun. Exposed as you are to this daily changing environment of light, temperature, and humidity, it follows that many of your organs and habits are adjusted to a twenty-four-hour schedule. However, like the thermostat in your furnace, the alarm on your clock-radio, and the control on your food freezer, they don't necessarily function simultaneously.

Your liver, soft, solid, reddish brown, and unglamorous, is one of the most important organs in your body. It performs at least 500 separate functions for you. Without it you would live only a few days at most. It has a fascinating twenty-four-hour cycle. During the day, while you are awake, it produces bile, which helps to emulsify and digest fat. At night, while you are resting, it breaks down glycogen into the glucose that you will need for energy to be your dynamic self when you awake.

Your blood pressure follows another metronome. It is at its lowest at about three in the morning; by three in the afternoon it has reached its highest reading.

During the night the vital capacity of your lungs decreases, while adrenaline, your body's activity-boosting hormone, is produced in its largest quantities between 4 and 6 A.M., just before you awake. By late evening you are producing little, if any, adrenaline.

You sleep in a twenty-four-hour rhythm, and your body temperature increases and decreases in a similar cycle. Your temperature reading will reach its peak during your waking hours and its lowest point comes while you are sleeping. As your temperature rises during the day, your efficiency increases; as it drops, so will your effectiveness. However, we are complicated and individualistic machines—not produced on any assembly line. We are different from each other in countless ways less visible than the pigment of our skin or the color of our eyes.

Some of us are "morning" people; others are "night" people. If you are a "morning" type, you will have your highest temperature early in the day and will do your best work during those hours. If you are an "evening" type—if you "hate to get up in the morning"— you will show a rising body temperature curve during the day and your greatest period of productivity is reached at just about the time when the "morning"' types are thinking about calling it a day.

If you are willing to risk creating among your fellow workers the impression that you are a hypochondriac, you can learn, within a very few weeks, whether you fall into the "morning" or "evening" category. Take your temperature, every hour, from the time you arise until you retire. If your temperature climbs as the day progresses, you are an "evening" person; if it decreases instead, perhaps you should plan your heavier work load for the first half of each day for you are the "morning" type.

Your twenty-four-hour temperature cycle tends to resist radical modification. Experiments seeking to find the answer to why people sleep and why the rhythm of sleep is twenty-four hours long have shown that while the pattern may be forcibly changed for a short period of time to a twenty-one-hour or even twenty-seven-hour rhythm, the twenty-four-hour temperature cycle refuses to go along with any alteration in sleep habits.

THE TIME ZONE SYNDROME

Now that we can fly around our planet in several hours, our commercial airline pilots are complaining about a new problem—time zone fatigue. They maintain, and correctly so, that although they have crossed several time zones, their body is still functioning on their home zone schedule, while at their place of landing everyone is living on a different schedule. The pilots want longer rest periods following lengthy transmeridian flights to give their body processes time to adjust to the new environment.

Many companies are now advising their executives not to perform any important business functions after crossing several time zones until they have rested for a day or more. Bad decisions, made under conditions of fatigue and altered body timetables, can be far more costly than an additional day or two of rest charged to the expense account. This point was dramatically made during Premier Kosygin's visit to the United States in 1967. Following his flight from Russia he refused to meet with the press or any members of the American government until he had rested for a week to allow his body "clocks" to adjust to the different time zone.

BODY "CLOCKS": FACT OR ILLUSION?

The scientific and medical debate as to whether all living organisms, including man, contain biological "clocks" that regulate body functions is not resolved. One group maintains that these "clocks" (still not located, if they do exist) are strictly internal devices uninfluenced from the outside.

Another group of biologists has performed experiments that do more than hint that nature's timetables, including man's, are affected by outside forces. Prominent in this area is the research being performed by Frank A. Brown, Jr., Morrison Professor of the Biological Sciences at Northwestern University.

One of Professor Brown's early experiments, in 1957, strengthened the "outside force" hypothesis. He collected a number of oysters from the seashore at New Haven, Connecticut, and transported them nearly a thousand miles to his laboratory in Evanston, Illinois. If those who maintained that all living organisms have internal "clocks" were correct, then the oysters—living in darkness in *covered* containers of Atlantic Ocean salt water, under constant conditions of temperature—should have opened their valves in Evanston at the same time as they always had at New Haven, in synchrony with the tides on their old seashore habitat.

They did just that—for a few days. But within two weeks they were opening and closing their valves at a different time, in synchrony with the positions of the moon in Evanston! The positions of the moon always coincide with the ebb and flow of atmospheric tides everywhere in the world, but there is no ocean tide in Evanston, Illinois. Yet the oysters, still covered, were synchronizing their movements with a nonexistent ocean tide that

45

"something" (certainly not any internal "clock") was telling them existed in their new neighborhood.

Professor Brown and his associates went further in their brilliant research. They began to experiment with a biological process common to every living thing—metabolism. Metabolism, in simplified, nonscientific terminology, is the measurement of chemical change in a living organism between the time it has been "fed" and the time it discharges the food as waste. Your physician might give you a "basal metabolism test" to discover whether or not your body is making proper use of the food it receives.

The subjects selected by Professor Brown were small pieces of potatoes with sprouting eyes. These young specimens were hermetically sealed, in constant darkness and *under constant conditions of pressure*, with proper recording apparatus to measure the rate at which the young sprouts consumed oxygen. Brown and his associates discovered that the potato had a twenty-four-hour cycle of oxygen consumption, even under these controlled conditions, which, evidence indicated, was somehow related to a similar twenty-four-hour cycle in barometric pressure outside its sealed container. Most surprising was the potato's ability to predict the outside barometric pressure *two days in advance*. The height of its afternoon peak in metabolic rate appeared to be related to the barometric pressure of the area two days later!

As Dr. Brown sums it up: "Every living thing studied in our laboratory, from carrots to seaweeds, and from crabs to oysters to rats...has shown this capacity to predict very safely, beyond chance, the barometric pressure changes usually two days in advance. It is interesting to contemplate the problem of a meteorologist sealed, incommunicado, for weeks or months in constant conditions, and asked to give two-day weather predictions... or for that matter, even to tell you the weather today."

Just as radio waves penetrate the walls of your home to bring you the six o'clock news, "something out there" penetrated hermetically sealed containers and triggered the strange and cyclic actions of Professor Brown's potatoes. You and I, of course, are not protected within sealed containers, nor do we go about our daily lives under constant conditions of temperature, humidity, and pressure. Yet we all would like to think that we are at least as sensitive as a potato. Do we then dare conclude that the same unknown forces that act on the oyster and the potato might also affect us? Could whatever force that "triggers" them also "trigger" some sensitive mechanism within us, causing our moods to fluctuate with all the characteristics of a barometer?

YOUR EMOTIONAL CYCLE

All of us have our emotional ups and downs. Some days we are riding the crest of elation, enthusiasm, and excitement. On those occasions we feel that there is nothing in the world that we cannot handle.

On other days we are "down in the dumps." The slightest remark will irritate us, our appetite is terrible, and we balloon the most insignificant situation completely out of proportion. Our attitude actually seems to attract trouble during this period.

Some years ago a scientific study of these emotional fluctuations in male human beings was conducted by Professor Rex Hersey of the University of Pennsylvania. His conclusion was that although the emotional cycles of individual men vary with the individual from sixteen days to sixty-three days, the average length for men is about five weeks. This is the typical length of time it takes for a normal man to move from one period of elation down the scale to a feeling of worry (the most destructive emotion, according to Hersey) and back up again to the next period of elation.

Professor Hersey and his group devoted an entire year to the observation of a group of normal workers of various occupations, ages, personality types, and ethnic backgrounds. Their behavior in countless areas, such as efficiency, productivity, cooperativeness, verbal outbursts, ideas, absenteeism, emotion, and reverie, was studied along with their blood pressure, weight, hours of sleep, feelings of fatigue, and illnesses.

To simplify and portray the fluctuating moods of his subjects, Professor Hersey constructed a scale of emotions to which he applied numerical values. Happiness and elation received the highest value, plus 6; worry was assigned the lowest value, minus 6.

Each day for thirteen weeks the subjects were briefly interviewed four times and given a "mood rating" for that day, ranging from plus 6 to minus 6. In most cases Professor Hersey believed that the subject's own opinion of how he felt combined with the interviewer's observation resulted in a fairly objective rating. Although such a method could never fathom or portray all the different emotions of an individual, it did chart, with sufficient accuracy, the dominant mood of the day.

The major surprise to Hersey was that although different individuals had different cycle lengths, they were always fairly constant for that individual. If one worker had an average mood cycle of five weeks, it was almost never less than four weeks, almost never more than six. In spite of domestic squabbles, trouble with the boss, great pleasures, promotions, job problems, unforeseen good luck, and accidents, this cycle *did not vary by more than one week from the normal cycle for that person.*

What are the symptoms of a high period in your emotional cycle? You bounce out of bed, hurry to work with enthusiasm, and tackle jobs that you have been putting off for days or weeks. Problems will stimulate you and no job is too difficult to tackle. You feel so great, physically, that when you return home from work you are ready for some social life. You also make plans for the future and think about that new automobile or a new house you want to buy. Financial problems almost disappear from your mind. You have what my good friend W. Clement Stone calls "a positive mental attitude."

In your low periods even going to work is an almost impossible task. Solving problems, or for that matter, any mental or physical effort, is difficult. You feel tired, depressed, and you worry about matters that you ignored during your "high" period. You become concerned about your job, your future, your family, your bank account, and your own health. You are negative in all your thinking.

Strange as it may seem, your sexual activity is probably greater during your "low" period. Since you are restless and sleep comes with difficulty, you will often engage in intercourse to quiet you and put you to sleep.

HOW TO FORECAST YOUR EMOTIONAL CYCLE

Obviously it would be of great help to you if you knew your "high" and "low" periods—and this can be quite easily learned, with a minimum of time. Begin by preparing a simple chart similar to the one shown in Figure 5.

Fig. 5: A Grid for Recording Your Emotions

MONTH		1	2	3	4	5	6	7	8	9	10	
Elated	+3											
Happy	+2											
Pleasant feeling	+1											
Neutral	0											
Unpleasant feeling	-1											
Disgusted; sad	-2											
Worried, depressed	-3											

Set up graph for 30 days

This is a simplified version of the graph used by Professor Hersey but it is sufficient to chart your own emotional cycle. Every evening take a few moments and review your general mood of the day. Then place a dot in the box which you believe most aptly defines your state of mind. Connect the dots with a straight line as time goes on.

Soon a pattern will emerge. This is your natural mood rhythm and in most cases it will continue. After a few months you will know, with amazing accuracy, when your next "high" is due and when you should prepare for your next "low." As I mentioned earlier, this cycle will normally not vary by more than one week either way. With this knowledge, this ability to at least partially "see into your future," you will be able to adjust your behavior to suit your mood. When you are going through your high period of elation, you will think twice before making rash promises, impossible commitments, or misguided installment purchases. You will also be able to live through your low periods of sadness and depression because you will know that these too will pass, within a few days. A greater knowledge of cycles, as you can see, will help you to change what can be changed and prepare for what cannot.

THE LOVE CYCLE

The female of our species also has an emotional cycle of approximately five weeks, but hers is complicated by two other cycles. With one, the menstrual cycle, she is quite familiar, for she has lived with it since the onset of her puberty and, except for periods of pregnancy, she is confronted with this cycle approximately every twenty-eight days. During this period, each month, especially if pain accompanies menstruation, the female is liable to varying moods of emotion.

But women have another cycle, little known to most, and first recorded in the 1930's by Dr. Marie Stopes—a fourteen-day cycle of amorousness. Dr. Stopes called her cycle "The Law of Periodicity of Recurrence of Desire in Women" (one wonders what it would be called today). After considerable research Dr. Stopes disclosed that normal women have a decided increase in their sexual desire just before menstruation begins and again eight or nine days after the cessation of the menstrual flow—a cycle of fourteen days. She also pointed out that the second increase in ardor, following the cessation of menstruation by eight or nine days, is exactly in agreement with the old Jewish plan of having twelve clear days after the beginning of menstruation before the next union should take place.

Obviously, then, if you are a woman and begin to keep your emotional chart as outlined here, there will be irregularities in its original appearance not found in the cycle of a male. Nevertheless, you will discover that in spite of these interruptions, both physical and psychological, you, too, have an emotional cycle that is approximately five weeks in length.

Why do our moods fluctuate in cycles? Professor Hersey thought that climate might be the cause but realized that there was no relationship between the cycles and climate conditions unless each person responded differently to changes in the weather, for each individual had his own cycle, which did not move up and down in the same wave as those of others.

His conclusion? He wrote, "Since there is no other single influence, besides climate, of which we have knowledge, that affects us all so equally without reference to individual conditions, one can only conclude that the basic cause of this very interesting human phenomenon is yet to be found. . ."

YOUR CYCLE OF CREATIVITY

Perhaps you can recall at least one instance when your memory or your ability to express yourself intelligently failed you in an interview or examination and possibly prevented you from obtaining a promotion, a big sale, or a job you wanted. You insist that if you had a second opportunity, you wouldn't fail—and you are very possibly correct. You may have failed on that particular day because you were in your low period of creativity.

Great writers, artists, musicians, and even scientists have long felt that their best work was performed in spurts, followed by long gaps of nonproductiveness. Unless they were "in the mood," they were completely impotent, artistically speaking.

Dr. J. H. Douglas Webster, whose chief contributions to the knowledge of rhythmic fluctuations are in the field of medicine, applied his brilliant analytical mind to exploring the possibility of cycles in creativity. His comprehensive research involved not only the assembling of data from the biographies and collected works of musicians and poets, but also a thorough review of earlier papers on the subject. The most prominent cycle he discovered in creativity averaged 7.6 months in length.

Where there were daily records available through diaries and letters it was discovered that Christina Rossetti, Anne Brontë, Johann Wolfgang von Goethe, August Platen, Heinrich Schütz, and Franz Schubert had peaks of creativity approximately every 7.6 months. Where there were monthly records available the same 7.6-month high in creativity was found in Rupert Brooke, John Keats, Percy Bysshe Shelley, Thomas Gray, Victor Hugo, Wolfgang Amadeus Mozart, Nikolai Andreevich Rimski-Korsakov, Pëtr Ilich Tchaikovsky, and Jean Sibelius. A similar cycle was discovered in the productiveness of Walter Scott, Katherine Mansfield, Gustave Flaubert, Henrik Ibsen, Richard Wagner, Charles Darwin, Claude Bernard, and Michael Faraday.

A longer cycle, seven years in length, was first noted by Pythagoras and later discussed by Cicero and Seneca. Sigmund Freud believed that his best periods of productivity came every seven years.

How many truly creative people would be relieved if they

8

realized—and learned to live with—the fact that their barren periods do not indicate that they are losing their touch but are instead only the inevitable "lows" of a cycle that will eventually take them into another "high" period of creativity? Here, indeed, is a subject fertile for further research and exploration.

YOUR ELECTRICAL CYCLE

Remember those trees in New Haven that produced electrical voltages in regular cycles?

All matter is fundamentally electric in nature. The paper on which these words are printed, the chair on which you are resting comfortably, the bed on which you will sleep—all are composed of negatively charged electrons circling constantly around positively charged protons. Now don't let this scientific terminology frighten you away. I merely want to remind you that our Connecticut trees with their electric voltage are composed of matter—and so are you.

Along the nerve fibers of your body direct electric current flows to transmit signals from your senses to the brain. Touch a hot stove with your hand and the sense of touch in your fingers will immediately flash a message via electric current back to your brain. Another message, almost simultaneously, will flash back from your brain down the nerves of your arm telling the muscles of your arm to remove the hand, quickly, from the hot stove. The flow of this electric current, similar to that in the tree, can be measured, and over 30,000 such measurements were made by Dr. Leonard Ravitz on almost 500 students at Yale University, Duke University, and the University of Pennsylvania.

Dr. Ravitz discovered that although we are subject to many different and periodic electric tides that sweep through our bodies daily, these tides, for the most part, *occur in cycles*. He noted a cycle of twenty-four hours and others of bimonthly, quarterly, and semiannual length. Need I remind you of the semiannual, or six-month, cycle also found in the voltage output of our trees?

THE AFTERSHOCK

One of the enigmas of cycle study is that individual human beings, plants, and animals have cycle lengths that are different from others in their group. Why is my emotional cycle five weeks long while yours is six weeks? Why does your "high" come at a time when I am at my "low"? Why am I a "morning" person while you do your best work in the evening?

Are there inherent differences in plants, animals, and human beings that determine their individual responsiveness to outside forces? Consider the pigments of an artist's palette. The red paint he applies to his canvas is exposed to the blue in the sunlight just as much as the blue paint, but it "elects" to respond only to the red rays of the spectrum. His blue paint is exposed to the red rays as much as the red pigment but it ignores the red rays and reflects only the blue. Could plants, animals, and human beings be similarly constituted?

The possibility of inherent differences in all of us was suggested by the work of Louis S. Goldstein, a pediatrician of Yonkers, New York, who has spent considerable time on the subject of "aftershock."

The first shock that we experience is the shock of being born. Sometime after birth, and later on after intrusions into our flesh such as operations and vaccinations, many of us experience what is known as a secondary shock or aftershock. If there are such things as "aftershock," wouldn't you expect them to happen at random and not on schedule? Dr. Goldstein's work shows that these aftershocks manifest themselves only on certain particular days. In the 214 births which he studied, although twenty-six infants had secondary shock at eight-day intervals and thirty-five infants had secondary shock at ten-day intervals, not one single infant had aftershock at nine-day intervals! Although ten other infants had aftershock at twelve-day intervals and twenty-five at fourteen-day intervals, not one infant had aftershock at eleven-day or thirteen-day intervals. It would be extraordinarily difficult to obtain such results by a random distribution of 214 cases.

Moreover, the critical days in many instances seem to have a simple arithmetical relationship. Many secondary shocks occur eight days after birth; others twenty-four days after birth. Some shocks occur seven days after birth, or fourteen days, or twenty-one days. Is it possible that someday we will be classified according to the number of days it takes each of us, individually, to echo an initial shock? Is there a hint in Dr. Goldstein's work that may someday provide the key to understanding the differences between you and me, between your cycles and mine?

"Scientific knowledge must pass through three stages before it can reach full effectiveness. First, discovery by the experimental researcher and his statement of the laws based upon it. Second, publication of that discovery and the teaching that spreads the information. Finally, the application of the discovery to some useful purpose."

—Roger Burlingame

5

The Invisible
Messenger

INDIVIDUAL HUMAN BEINGS are distinctly different from each other, as you have seen.

But, in the mass, we all seem to march to the same drumbeat. We conform, almost as if an invisible messenger appears among us from time to time and gently whispers commands that we all proceed to follow blindly and without reason.

This is one of the most important lessons we can learn from history. Human beings, *in the mass*, have alternating periods of elation and depression. They become belligerent in cycles, producing wars, revolutions, and civil strife; this mass murder is then followed by periods of passiveness, constriction, and inaction.

At one period they will flock to the financial centers of the world and risk all their holdings on tulip bulbs, resort land, and that intangible called a stock certificate. At other times they are overwhelmed by plagues of doubt and they stampede to convert their assets into cash and gold.

During one swing of the millennium's pendulum they elevate creativity to a function approaching godliness. The artist, the musician, the poet, become the princes of heaven. Later, ambitions, instincts, and morality are submerged in the darkest of ages.

Why does our behavior alternate with such regularity?

EFFECT—OR CAUSE?

I lived through four years of college and well into the depression of the 1930's before I ever heard the word "depression" in connection with a business setback. The old word to describe this state of affairs was "panic." When I first heard the word "depression" I thought it was newly coined, but apt.

Sometime during that period, for some long-forgotten reason, I was reading through some 1875 and 1876 issues of the *New York Times* dealing with the severe hard times then being experienced in the wake of the 1873 panic. To my great surprise I noticed that they had used the word "depression" then. It wasn't new after all!

Are people depressed in a depression because business is poor? Or is business poor because people are depressed? I suspect it is the latter. Psychology defines depression as "an emotional state tending to general inactivity." What better term could be used to describe a state of mind that might bring about a business setback?

As a specific instance, I remember that in 1930, after a stroke from which he later died, my father was in what could be called a state of depression. He had lost some money in the 1929 stock market crash, and it had become urgent that he immediately lower his previous standard of living.

"Don't you realize that you must move to a cheaper apartment?" I asked.

"Yes," he mumbled.

"Do you understand that you cannot possibly afford to stay in this one?"

"Yes."

"Then, will you move?"

"No," he answered faintly.

"Why not?"

"I don't know."

He knew that he should move. He knew that he must move—and yet his power to act seemed to be paralyzed.

I conceive that human beings in the mass may be affected by forces in the environment which first elate them, then depress them. Their elation results in overexpansion; their depression, as in my father's case, results in inability to think logically or to act with any degree of common sense.

I also conceive that these forces, whatever they may be, also affect plant life, animal life, and our weather. That such forces do exist is based on the following chain of reasoning:

1. Almost everything fluctuates.
2. Many things fluctuate in cycles or waves.
3. Many of these waves (like our alternating red and black playing cards) repeat so regularly, so dominantly, and so many times, that they cannot possibly be accidental or ascribed to "chance."
4. If the wave, or cycle, is not repeating by chance, then something, some force, must "trigger" it.

When we discover the "force" or the "forces" we will have solved our mystery.

INTERNAL AND EXTERNAL CYCLES

After we have ruled out the possibility that a cycle we have discovered may be accidental, it must fall into one of two categories. The rhythm has either an internal or an external cause.

Internal rhythms come in two varieties: dynamic or feedback. Dynamic cycles are caused by actions within a system. Many of your bodily rhythms considered in the previous chapter are dynamic. Like your heartbeat they have no external cause. Heartbeats, of course, may be momentarily influenced by outside forces—a pretty girl or a tiger loose on the street—but the *rhythm* is not controlled externally.

Prices too may have internal or dynamic cycles. The price of gumbos begins to climb. People note this and overbuy to protect themselves. Then gumbos are no longer needed, for everyone is overstocked. The demand slackens. Prices falter and begin to fall. People, seeing the falling prices, hold off from buying in expectation of even lower prices. Prices eventually get too low and gumbos become a bargain. People begin to buy, prices rise, and the cycle starts over again.

Many of these dynamic cycles are of the utmost importance to specific branches of medicine, economics, and science. However, their existence and cause are known, for the most part, and in the study of cycles as such they are little more than curiosities.

Closely related to the dynamic cycles is the feedback group. To understand feedback consider the relationship between your furnace and its thermostat. When the air in your home becomes too cool, the thermostat clicks and the furnace blazes into action. When your house becomes warm, the thermostat shuts off and your house begins to cool, causing the cycle to repeat.

Another form of feedback cycle is the predator–prey relationship. Let us imagine that a certain type of bird can eat only a certain insect and this specific insect is eaten only by this type of bird. We begin with many birds and many insects. The birds have plenty of food and so they multiply. As the bird population increases, the insects get pretty well eaten up. Then, with no food, the birds die off. Now the insects have a chance and they begin to multiply. The birds have food again. They begin to multiply, and the cycle starts over. Under fairly constant conditions, the time intervals between the highs in this particular bird population can be very regular.

Also, under reasonable conditions of uniformity, closed doors, closed windows, and a constant outside temperature, the intervals between our furnace going on can be fairly regular—a cycle.

All dynamic and feedback cycles have characteristics that indicate they are not triggered by outside forces. The only sort of rhythm that commands our attention is the sort that could *conceivably* have an external cause—a forced cycle.

Forced cycles are those where the regulating mechanism—the "trigger"—appears to be outside the system. You are *forced* to arise every morning because the rotation of the earth on its axis produces night and day. You are *forced* to put antifreeze in your car when winter approaches and you are *forced* to wear cooler and lighter clothing in the heat of summer.

I am using the word "forced" in the technical rather than popular sense. Obviously, unless you have a very unusual wife, no one will hold a gun to your head to force you to arise in the morning. You don't *have* to get out of bed because daylight has appeared. Theoretically at least you can lie in bed as late as you like or as long as you like—several hours, days, months, or even years. But when you do resume getting up in the morning it will be at some multiple of twenty-four hours from the time you did it last. Your twenty-four-hour cycle has continued as a force whether you have been responding to it or not, and when you finally do respond, the timing is set for you by outside forces. It is the same with the cycles of other lengths with which this book is largely concerned.

To be able to distinguish between accidental, internal, and external cycles is of prime importance. If the cycle is accidental, we know it will not continue. If for three successions every fourth car you pass on the highway is a Volkswagen, it does not follow that three cars later you will pass another Volkswagen, except by accident.

At the other end of the scale: Even if you don't know the cause, you can count on the 12½-hour cycle of the tides, the twenty-four-hour cycle of the day, the twenty-five-hour cycle of the moon, the seven-day cycle of the week (man-made to be sure, but a forced cycle, nevertheless), and the twelve-month cycle of the year.

Between these two extremes is the great body of rhythmic cycles, any one of which may be accidental or dynamic or feedback or forced. If a cycle is accidental, it has, of course, no forecasting value. If it is dynamic or feedback, it has some forecasting value. If it is forced, it has a great deal of forecasting value.

DO EXTERNAL FORCES EXIST?

Despite evidence accumulated through many years, the case for the existence of outside forces that may cause rhythmic cycles has yet to be proved. We do not *know* that forces of this sort surround us, and if they do exist, what they are. No one has ever seen them, for they are as invisible as radio waves. Few people have even considered their existence and we can only assume they exist from the behaviors we have observed.

Radio and radio waves offer an analogy that presents us with one possible, though partial, explanation of our mystery. Before I proceed, let me repeat the word "possible" so that there will be no misunderstanding between us. I am only putting our clues on the table for your inspection.

We all know about radios and, in a general way, how they operate. You are aware that the room in which you are now sitting is filled with radio waves. You can't see, hear, feel, or smell them, but you know they are there because whenever you turn on your radio the waves are converted into sound.

You also realize that these radio waves bouncing around your room are not identical. Each broadcasting station transmits waves with a different number of cycles per second, and your radio receiver will respond to one or another of these vibrations depending on where you set your dial.

Now imagine that a man from Mars is a guest in my house. He is a good physicist but he knows nothing about radio or broadcasting stations. He examines my radio and after some time he is able to determine that when he sets the dial at 79.4, the radio will vibrate 79.4 thousand times per second. When he sets my other radio in the next room to vibrate the same way, *it plays the same tune.*

With these facts it does not take our brilliant Martian long to reason that both rooms are filled with a vibration to which both radios respond and that somewhere there is something that causes these vibrations. When he moves both dials to 98.2 and then 101.4, the same thing happens . . . and he assumes there must be a second generating force, somewhere, vibrating at 98.2 thousand times per second and a third vibrating at 101.4 thousand times per second.

But he has absolutely no proof that these waves or their sending stations exist. He has deduced their existence logically through his observation of the behavior of the little black boxes!

Now suppose that my man from Mars, while awaiting dinner, comes across some statistics and papers in my library that indicate that every ten years or so Canadian lynx are more abundant, creating a rhythmic cycle of great regularity, with their population increasing for four or five years and then decreasing for an equal span of time. He also discovers that rainfall in London and rainfall in parts of India fluctuate in cycles of the same length, as does the abundance of ozone at Paris, the number of caterpillars in New Jersey, the abundance of salmon on both sides of the Atlantic, and many other phenomena. What's more, he learns that other things act as if they respond to forces with different time intervals—but still in cycles.

With all his Martian enthusiasm he exclaims, "This is amazing. What I have read is exactly like that radio thing—except that these different phenomena seem to be the receiving sets instead of those little black boxes. The black boxes vibrated in fractions of a second but there must be other external forces that vibrate in months and days and years instead of thousandths of a second."

"Now," he adds, "I shall ask my host to explain all this to me. He can tell me, I am sure, what makes the black boxes play the same tune when they are set at the same frequency. And he can also tell me what makes dozens and dozens of phenomena on this planet vibrate together as if they were all subject to the same force."

My friend from Mars overrates me. True, I can tell him something about radio waves and sending stations. I can explain "wavelength" as the physical distance, measured in meters, between two successive highs of radio waves. I can also describe "frequency" as the number of these waves, traveling at the speed of light, that will pass a given point in a second.

But for the longer cycles I have no explanation, no proof of their existence. All I can do is present for his consideration, and yours, the *probability* that our environment is pervaded by longer waves—perhaps of a similar basic nature as the radio waves—that, like their faster and smaller "brothers," cannot be seen, smelled, heard, or consciously felt. The crests of these longer waves, if they exist, might come at daily, weekly, monthly, even yearly intervals instead of thousandths of a second. And if they are similar to radio waves, their physical length will have to be measured in miles or even light-years instead of in meters.

No instrument of crystal, transistors, and wire, with dials and gauges, has yet been devised with sensitivity sufficient to detect and record these ultralong waves. We cannot prove their existence, we do not know their cause or nature, and we cannot pinpoint or even guess their points of origin. In the scientific sense they have not been reproduced or demonstrated in a laboratory and thus they are not recognized by scientific men of good will. And yet the circumstantial evidence that they exist is overwhelming, and we need only call Professor Brown's oysters and potatoes to the witness box to shake the unbending minds of dogmatic science.

If instruments cannot, as yet, detect these forces, how do we know that they exist? Because human beings, plants, and animals are apparently sensitive to them. We judge that they are sensitive to these forces because, *in the mass*, their behavior fluctuates in a way that could not be chance any more than the behavior of our alternating red and black playing cards.

Some will argue that these various events that occur in cycles behave as they do because of inbuilt reasons. They say that the cycles are dynamic or perhaps feedback. But they remain mute when asked to explain how Atlantic salmon, Canadian lynx, Indian rainfall, and Parisian ozone could *independently* and internally all possess what appears to be the same cycle. There is no thermostat–furnace relationship here by any possible stretch of the imagination.

POWER TO CHANGE THE WORLD

We have circled around our evidence and it remains an enigma. But if these regularities, or at least some of them, derive their rhythm from outside forces, and if these forces obey laws that man can discover and learn, our powers of prediction can change our world.

The implications within this possibility cannot be reviewed too often—for we will be able to forecast, with some accuracy, everything that is affected by these forces. Meteorologists, farmers, and sportsmen have been mentioned earlier, but many others who would benefit from the solution to our great cycle mystery come to mind. Bankers would know the probable increase and decrease of interest rates and general business activity. Manufacturers would be able to compute the probable increase and decrease in the demand for their products, adjust their production schedules, and avoid excessive inventories. The real estate gentry would have homes ready for occupancy when needed and avoid the costly construction of unwanted floor space. Investors would know, if they paused to take heed, when the prices of stocks and commodities were about to increase and when they were due to decline. Governments would know in advance when they were approaching a period of international tension and would be able to take suitable steps for appropriate defense. There is no phase of human activity that could not benefit from increased knowledge of the future.

Obviously if these forces do exist, and if they have influenced human affairs in the past, any theory of human activity that fails to take these forces into account is deficient. History, economics, philosophy, and every other area touched by man would need to be reevaluated. As one sociologist suggested, even sociology might become a science.

Circumstantial though it may be, our evidence that such forces do exist refuses to be swept into a closet. Pattern does exist, and something must act to create it, for in the absence of order the natural state of things is disorder. Witness a handful of iron filings thrown casually on the top of your desk. If the filings should fall into a pattern similar to that in Figure 6, you know that there must be a magnet hidden under the desk top.

Fig. 6: Lines of Force of a Bar Magnet

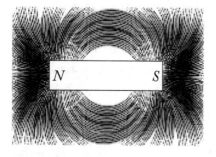 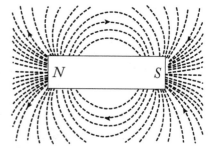

Even if you were an Aboriginal person who had never heard of magnets, you would know that *something* is at work to convert into order that which otherwise would be mere chance distribution.

THE CONSEQUENCES
OF PREDICTABILITY

Hopefully this has opened new vistas in your concept of cycles. Perhaps the possibility that man will eventually be able to predict the future quickens your pulse. On the other hand, you may have grave misgivings. The late Frederick H. Ecker, former Chairman of the Board of the Metropolitan Life Insurance Company, once spoke out on this point.

Mr. Ecker had been a guest at a luncheon given for me by Robert Struthers, who at that time was a senior partner of Wood, Struthers and Company, investment bankers. At the luncheon, naturally, I talked about cycles.

After the luncheon Mr. Ecker said to Mr. Struthers (as nearly as I can remember his words, repeated to me later by Mr. Struthers), "It's all right to play with this cycle business if you are sure there is nothing to it. But if you ever come to believe that this fellow Dewey has something, drop it like a hot potato. There would be nothing worse for the human race than to be able to know the future."

Probably Mr. Ecker meant that *complete* knowledge of the future would be bad for man. If so, I agree with him.

Suppose you had complete knowledge of your future. You would know everything that was going to happen from now to the end of your time in the world. Among other things you would know, if it were the case, that tomorrow afternoon you were going to be involved in an automobile accident which would kill you. Naturally, knowing the result of your forthcoming tragedy, you would not ride in an automobile tomorrow.

Now this would have many consequences. Your wife would not eventually marry the man from Peoria because she would not be a widow. Your assistant would not get that promotion because you would still be alive. Lacking the promotion, he would quit and move to Rochester, which he would not have done if you had died. He would have a child he would not otherwise have had. So would you. And so on. In time the cumulative sequence of events would change the whole course of history.

If you possessed this foreknowledge (unless you have more restraint than most of us), I am afraid you would exercise your powers for your own benefit, no matter how much it upset the plan and pattern of the universe.

But the study of cycles *can never give complete foreknowledge.* There will always be accidental variations and noncyclic factors that will enter into every situation, no matter how much we know about cycles.

When the caveman learned that winter and summer alternated with regularity he took a major stride forward in learning how to adjust to his environment. Thereafter in warm times of plenty he could lay up food and fuel for the cold times of want.

Is it too much to hope that a million years later we can learn and make use of cycles similar to our caveman's simple cycle of the year—but with other and more complex wavelengths?

"*A mob is usually a creature of very mysterious existence. . . . Where it comes from, or whither it goes, few men can tell. Assembling and dispersing with equal suddenness, it is as difficult to follow to its various sources as the sea itself; nor does the parallel stop here, for the ocean is no more fickle and uncertain, more terrible when roused, more unreasonable or more cruel.*"

—Charles Dickens

6

The Mob Cycles

THE WORD "MOB" traces its ancestry to the Latin *mobile vulgus*, the movable common people. Mobs come in various sizes and personalities. They can be lawless, disorderly, passive, angry, warlike, organized, leaderless, fanatic.

No severe stretching of the imagination is required to picture mankind, *in the mass*, as a mob, even in some of its more peaceful pursuits.

Emerson once wrote, "It seems as if heaven had sent its insane angels into our world as to an asylum. And here they will break out into their native music, and utter at intervals the words they have heard in heaven; then the mad fit returns and they mope and wallow like dogs." Why we act this way and what force triggers our actions, usually in cycles, is the purpose of this inquiry. Our investigation throughout the remainder of this book will focus on behavior *in the mass* rather than on individual phenomena. *We are searching for the forces that command the "movable common people."*

WE EXCITABLE HUMANS

Shortly after World War I a brilliant Russian, Professor A. L. Tchijevsky, published a book with a title guaranteed never to appear on any theater marquee: *Investigation of the Relationship Between the Sunspot Activity and the Course of the Universal Historical Process from the V Century B.C. to the Present Day*. Tchijevsky's premise was that disturbances on the sun—sunspots— which occur in greater number every eleven years, cause mass excitement here on earth.

First, of course, Tchijevsky had to show that mankind did, indeed, suffer periods of unrest every eleven years—a monumental task. The professor conducted long and detailed studies of the statistics and histories of seventy-two countries from 500 B.C. to 1922, a period of 2,422 years. He included in his compilations such signs of human unrest and excitability as wars, revolutions, riots, expeditions, and migrations, plus such factors as the number of humans involved, the quality of the event, and the size of area affected. The time when the unrest began and its high point were also reduced to arithmetical values of varying significance.

With his volumes of data Professor Tchijevsky constructed a year-by-year Index of Mass Human Excitability that covered the past twenty-four centuries in an amazing panorama of man's emotional moods (see Figure 7).

Fig. 7: Mass Human Excitability, 500 B.C.–A.D. 1922

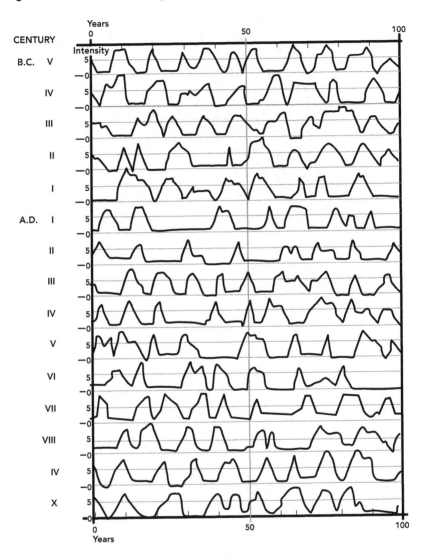

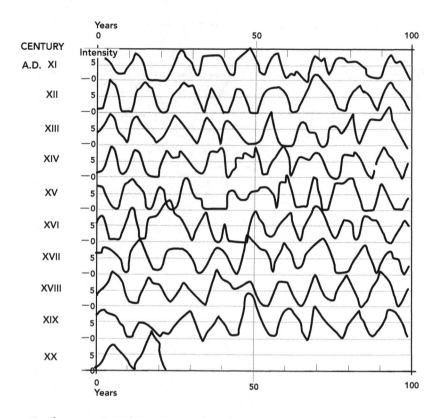

Professor A. L. Tchijevsky's Index of Mass Human Excitability. Note the tendency for nine waves in each century.

As you can see, the Index fluctuates in waves that tend to number about nine per century and, on the average, each wave is about 11.1 years long.

Tchijevsky's analysis indicated that each eleven-year cycle has four components. The first period, lasting approximately three years, has a minimum of excitability and is characterized by peace, tolerance, passiveness, lack of unity, and autocratic rule by minorities.

This is followed by a two-year period in which excitability grows. The masses begin to organize under new, revolutionary leaders. They challenge political and military decisions with new concepts, usually centering around one theme and encouraged by the press. Various leaders arise in local situations with no apparent loyalty or alliance uniting them with other pockets of unrest.

The third period, approximately three years in length, is one of maximum excitability, but one which solves the most pressing problems of the era. Often these outstanding achievements are accompanied by the strangest insanities. Revolutions and wars abound, splinter groups congeal under one hypnotic leader, great military, political, and spiritual leaders emerge, and the people's voice is heard. The masses riot, bloody conflicts are commonplace, and the old establishment, in a most paralyzed state of inaction, offers only feeble resistance and is destroyed. Anarchy prevails but the fruits of its action are democratic and social reforms.

The fourth period, approximately three years in length, witnesses a gradual decrease in excitability until the masses are almost inert and apathetic. "Peace" is their cry, and their unity, so evident during the struggle, disappears. They slumber, like a bear in hibernation, comalike, awaiting a new season, a new cycle.

Although Professor Tchijevsky's Index extends only through 1922 you might wish to place your finger on the bottom row, our twentieth century, and move it across to this current year. Then, although this would not be completely accurate, move your finger up the page to the corresponding time in other centuries, and make your own conclusions about the validity of Tchijevsky's work as it relates to the present.

Whether or not the good professor proved his hypothesis that sunspots cause our unrest is something we will explore later when we take a long look at our sun.

THE RHYTHMIC PROTESTANTS

One evening early in 1950 the phone rang in my home in Riverside, Connecticut. A pleasant voice said, "This is Harold Martin speaking. I am pastor of the First Congregational Church of Norwalk, Connecticut. I'd like to come to your office, whenever you can see me, to show you some charts I've made that show the fluctuations of new membership of various Protestant denominations and of various individual Protestant churches. New membership seems to go up and down in cycles, and I want your opinion in regard to what I've discovered."

"Of course," I said, "I'd be delighted." And so, in due course, Mr. Martin appeared.

He had completed a prodigious amount of work with charts of new members for the Methodist, Episcopal, Presbyterian, and Congregational denominations. His figures extended back to the very beginning of such figures, many well over one hundred years. He also had charts indicating the new membership of many individual churches.

The first thing that Mr. Martin had discovered was that, regardless of location, there is a tendency for additions to membership to go up and down together. For example, when people were flocking to join the Congregational churches in Boston, they were also flocking to join the Congregational churches in Norwalk, San Francisco, and Seattle.

This national movement puzzled Mr. Martin, for he had always believed that church membership increased or decreased in accordance with local situations. Undoubtedly local influences are important, but Mr. Martin's work indicated that there were larger forces, at least national in scope, that were also at work, and the national forces seemed to have more strength and influence than the local forces.

Here was something with startling potential significance to

evangelism in the churches. For if the forces that lead people to church membership are not local, churchmen must discover what these forces are and turn this information to use in expanding their flocks.

The second discovery made by Mr. Martin was that additions to membership in different Protestant denominations went up and down more or less together. At times when great numbers of people were joining Congregational churches, great numbers were also joining the Methodist church, the Episcopal church, and the Presbyterian church. Possibly he might have discovered this same movement in the Catholic and Jewish faiths had he also studied their figures, although I have no data on which to base my assumption.

The simultaneous movement toward denominations as such also surprised Mr. Martin. He had assumed that increases in Methodist membership would coincide with the coming of great Methodist evangelists and that increases in Presbyterian membership would coincide with the coming of great Presbyterian leaders. And indeed, in the record, one can see the influence of great individuals. But beyond this one can also note general patterns of ebb and flow that seem *to affect all denominations simultaneously*. These basic forces seem to operate not only independently of geography but also independently of creed.

Finally, Mr. Martin made a third discovery, and it was this observation that brought him to Foundation headquarters. He discovered that at least some of the ups and downs of new membership in the various churches showed rhythm. There was a tendency for man to "return to God" every nine years—in a cycle (see Figure 8).

As you study these three charts here is an excellent opportunity for me to show you how we locate a possible cycle. Although I must warn you that this is an extremely simplified version of the technique involved, you might wish to experiment with other figures of your own, such as the annual sales of your company.

Figure 8a is a chart of the actual new membership in the Presbyterian church in this country. In 1826 the new membership was 12,938; by 1831 it had climbed to 34,160; then it dipped to 23,546 in 1832, etc. You've seen hundreds of charts like this: charts of the stock market, weather charts, perhaps charts of your company's sales volume. Although you can see some highs and lows that stand out on the chart, it is fairly difficult to spot any regularity in the rhythm.

So, like the scientist in his laboratory, we proceed to extract the impurities and the irregularities in our chart. We do this by means of a moving average. We take the new membership figures for 1826, 1827, and 1828 and average them. This average for the three years is plotted in Figure 8b for the middle year, 1827. Then we take the figures for 1827, 1828, and 1829 and average them. This average figure for three years is plotted on Figure 8b for 1828. We continue across the years, and now we have a line, the heavy unbroken one in Figure 8b, that is smoother and that lacks many "impurities." However, any hints of a regular rhythm are still misty.

Now we refine even further to obtain a trend line. "Trend" is the general direction in which our series of figures is headed, either up, or down, or sideways. It smooths out the violent fluctuations of yearly new membership simply by taking, in this case, a nine-year moving average similar to the three-year one we mentioned above. The dotted line in Figure 8b is our "trend" line.

Now we're getting close to the payoff.

Fig. 8: Presbyterian Church New Membership, 1826–1948

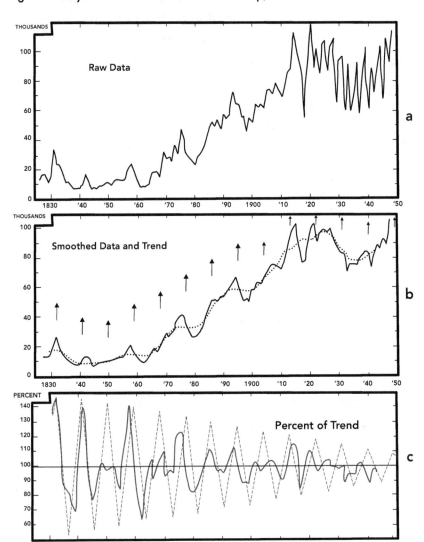

New membership of the Presbyterian Church in the U.S.A. (northern) through profession and reaffirmation of faith.

Note that Figure 8c has percentage values, whereas Figures 8a and 8b indicated the numbers, in thousands, of new memberships. All we do, in Figure 8c, is plot the percentage that each point of our three-year moving average (solid line) is above or below the corresponding value of our dotted trend line in Figure 8b.

One example should clarify this. New members in 1830, 1831, and 1832 were 15,357, 34,160, and 23,546, respectively—a three-year average of 24,354. This is the value that was plotted for 1831, on Figure 8b, as part of our solid line. Note that this figure for 1831 (24,354) is higher than our trend or dotted line for 1831, whose figure for that year is 17,974. Thus, our three-year moving average, 24,354 in 1831, was 135 percent of our trend, 17,974, and this we plot for 1831 in Figure 8c. As we do this for each year, we are plotting deviation (departure), up or down, from our dotted trend line, and an apparent cycle begins to take shape before our eyes. To help you see it I have drawn an exact nine-year cycle in a broken zigzag line on Figure 8c.

The figures used were adjusted to allow for their change in record keeping from a fiscal year to a calendar year in 1947.

Figure 9 is similar to Figure 8c, showing a similar nine-year cycle in new membership of the Congregational churches.

Fig. 9: Congregational Church New Membership, 1861–1950

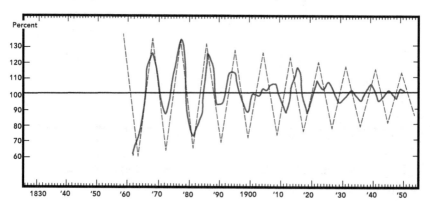

New membership of the Congregational Church, smoothed, shown as amounts above or below trend. Compare this chart with Figure 8, which shows similar behavior in Presbyterian Church new membership.

As you can see, when comparing Figure 9 with Figure 8c, the time of ideal crests for numbers of new Presbyterians and new Congregationalists is *identical*, although the fluctuations in both are of much less percentage importance than they once were.

This nine-year cycle, by the way, is nearly directly opposite to the timing of another cycle of similar length—in bank deposits, cotton prices, Canadian Pacific Railway ton-miles, and other business indicators. Why is this church membership rhythm of the same length as one of the main rhythms in economics, but upside-down? Why do more people join churches in nine-year intervals and why is this rhythm of less strength than before while the rhythm in economics continues with vitality? No one knows, but perhaps these questions are related to our earlier thoughts. Could there be something that makes us alternately bold and fearful at intervals of about nine years?

If so, when we are bold and self-sufficient, might we not be concerned with business and raise prices by bidding against each other? And when we are fearful, might we not be more apt to join a church? This idea would fit into the decreasing importance of the nine-year wave in church membership, for everyone knows that over the past fifty years Protestants have been generally much less afraid of eternal fire and damnation than were their grandfathers and great-grandfathers.

Nevertheless, a 1967 Gallup poll indicated that church attendance increased during 1967 to 45 percent of the adult population. The last peak year, according to the report, was 1958, when 49 percent attended during a typical week. Peak years for our nine-year cycle in new church membership, according to the average cycle, were 1940, 1949, 1958... and 1967! The cycle continues.

THE CURVE OF CONSCIENCE

Closely related to church membership, or at least to some of the Ten Commandments preached by most churches, is the matter of mass conscience, for even here we find a cycle.

One measure of conscience *in the mass* is provided by the voluntary guilt offerings made by British taxpayers covering a period of thirty-two years from 1923 to 1954. Each year the Chancellor of the Exchequer enters these unexplained and anonymous receipts under the heading of "Conscience money, remitted by sundry persons for conscience' sake." Figure 10 clearly shows a cycle that averages 3½ years from peak to peak.

Fig. 10: The Cycle of Guilt, 1923–54

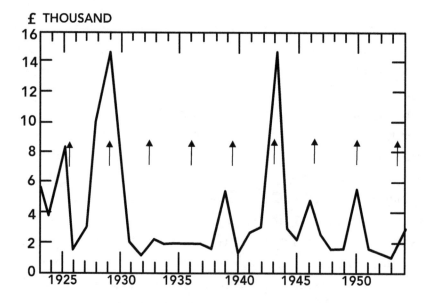

A 3½-year cycle in "conscience money" or guilt offerings remitted by British taxpayers, in thousands of pounds. Arrows are spaced at 3½-year intervals.

Unfortunately the "curve of conscience" graph depicts the guilt offerings in money instead of in number of persons making payments. Otherwise the peaks might be nearer in size to each other, but in any event, despite the variation of amplitude (a word used to describe the height or depth of a wave), the regularity of timing is clearly visible.

Could this regularity be the result of chance? Yes, but with eight waves as regularly spaced as these it could not *easily* be the result of chance. Do we know that these guilt offerings are really the result of a 3½-year cycle in the pricks of conscience? Not necessarily. The payments might be a result of a cycle in the ability to pay. Something, however, did cause the behavior, and the behavior is cyclic.

MARRIAGE, DEATH, AND THE BUSTLE

Two of the most important activities of man *in the mass* are his predilection to fight and to speculate. Because both of these movements affect our lives so greatly, we will deal with them in separate chapters.

But there are countless other important cycles of mankind, and the author's problem becomes one of space and selectivity. Which, of thousands, do I parade before your reviewing stand? Which, of thousands, do I allow to remain in the Foundation's files for a second book, and a third?

Variety, I believe, is the ultimate solution. I will select examples from the widest possible spectrum of our research so that the universality of rhythmic cycles becomes an acceptable fact of life to you.

The magic spell of love, so sings the poet, is everywhere. But if marriage is the ultimate expression of love, then the magic spell must increase every 18.2 years, for there has been a definite marriage cycle of this length in our country.

When we studied this phenomenon in 1955, estimates of marriages per 1,000 of population were available from 1867 through 1953. Although the recent trend in the number of marriages is up, the 18.2-year cycle is obvious in Figure 11. There was a high percentage of marriages during the years of World War II and immediately after, but the rhythm corrected itself by 1950. There is no explanation for this cycle.

Although our death rate is decreasing at a rate guaranteed to warm any insurance company's actuarial heart, we apparently die in a cycle. Data covering the death rate in Massachusetts from 1860 through 1962 have been analyzed. A cycle of 8.92 years was indicated (see Figure 12).

From death, we cut through sociological barriers to consider the shape of women's evening dresses. Studies by Agnes Brooks Young that cover the period from 1725 to the present show that three basic designs, bell-shaped, backsided or bustle, and tubular, tend to succeed each other at about thirty-five-year intervals and come full cycle in 105 years. We are currently in the "bell-shaped" era and should see the return of the "bustle" by the mid 1970's.

Fig. 11: The 18.2-Year Cycle in Marriage Rates in the United States, 1869–1951

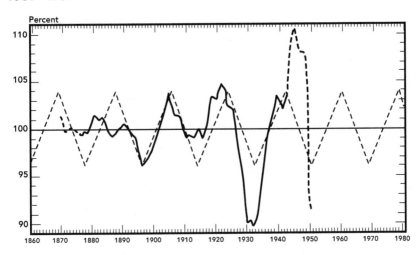

Note: All charts throughout the remainder of this book will show the cycle under discussion as amounts above and below trend unless otherwise specified.

Fig. 12: The 8.9-Year Cycle in Death Rates in Massachusetts, 1865–1961

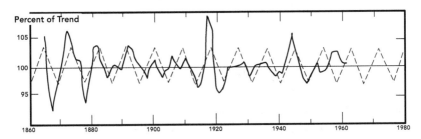

By the way, all girl watchers will be interested to learn that skirt lengths seem to go up and down in a cycle of one hundred years, while décolletage has a cycle of its own—it hides and then exposes in a seventy-one-year rhythm.

While we are on a lighter note, consider eyeglasses. In the

1920's the squared-off steel frame was fashionable. Then someone developed a frame slanted upward and outward to two points, called it the "harlequin," and began to adorn our glasses with everything from sequins to leopard spots. Now, to be "in," your eyeglass frame must be plain and unadorned, and even the round glasses of colonial days are considered chic.

A member of the Foundation once wrote me about the yo-yo. He had a friend in the wholesale toy business who dreaded the advent of the yo-yo fad every few years. When the fad hit, he would find it nearly impossible to maintain a supply large enough to meet the demand of retail stores. Then one morning, with no advance notice, the demand for yo-yo's would have evaporated completely.

We don't know why the desire to buy yo-yo's vanishes over a wide area at the same time, but I suspect that if we did know, it might throw some light on the subject of cycles. Buyers of tin tell me that a similar reversal of attitude in respect to future tin prices suddenly occurs on the part of a variety of brokers for no apparent reason. I have also been told that the popularity of particular kinds of games, such as Monopoly, recurs at intervals of about fourteen years. Perhaps someday we will know why the popularity of these things fluctuates.

THE TIRED MASSES

Although the United States is a country composed almost entirely of immigrants and their descendants, immigration has always been a political football. First we open our gates and the refugees swarm in. Then we panic and legislate quotas for each country. Then we relax the quotas, etc., etc. But in spite of all this tinkering with our immigration laws, the people of the world still come to us for freedom from poverty, religious persecution, and oppression—and they do so in a cycle that has averaged 18.2 years since the early nineteenth century (see Figure 13).

Fig. 13: The 18.2-Year Cycle of Immigration into the United States, 1824–1950

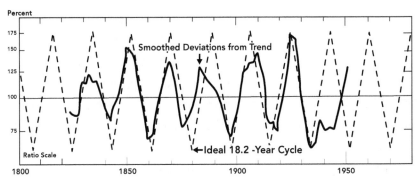

A cycle length of 18.2 years is exactly the same as what we just mentioned in marriages, and if you compare the two graphs you will note that they seem to go up and down at the same time. The same cycle length of 18.2 or 18.3 years is evident in industrial common stocks, real estate activity, wheat acreage, freight traffic on the Canadian Pacific Railway, lumber and furniture production, floods on the Nile, tree rings in Java, and many more. What is it out there that makes all these unrelated phenomena vibrate with the same rhythm?

"THE CRIME OF THE MONTH"

Crime, J. Edgar Hoover reported in *This Week Magazine* some years ago, has its own cycles, and police records tabulated for five years from over 2,400 cities and towns show a startling link between seasonal changes and crime patterns. Mr. Hoover indicated that meteorologists, to a limited extent, could predict rapes as well as hurricanes (see Figure 14).

The pattern of crime has varied very little over a long period of years. Murder reaches its high during July and August, as do rape and aggravated assault. Murder, moreover, is more than seasonal;

it's a weekend crime. It's also a nighttime crime: 62 percent of murders are committed between 6 P.M. and 6 A.M.

Unlike the summer high in crimes of bodily harm, burglary has a different cycle. You are most likely to be robbed between 6 P.M. and 2 A.M. on a Saturday night in December, January, or February.

The most uncriminal month of all? May—except for one strange statistic. More dog bites are reported in this merry month than any other month of the year, including the torrid "dog days" of July and August.

Apparently our intellectual seasonal cycles are completely different from our criminal tendencies. Professor Huntington, until his death a valued board member of the Foundation for the Study of Cycles, made extensive studies to discover the seasons when people read serious books, attend scientific meetings, make the highest scores on examinations, and file the most amendments to patents. In all instances he found a spring peak and an autumn peak separated by a summer low.

Conversely, Professor Huntington's studies indicated that June is the peak month for suicides and admissions to mental hospitals. (It is also the peak month for marriages, although I leave any possible correlation to someone braver than I.)

Possibly, soaring thermometers and stifling humidity are the catalysts that bring on our strange and terrifying summer actions, but J. Edgar Hoover is not sure. He says, "There is, of course, no proof of a correlation between humidity and homicide. Why murder's high tide should come in summertime we frankly don't know."

Fig. 14: Annual Cycles of Crime (after Hoover)

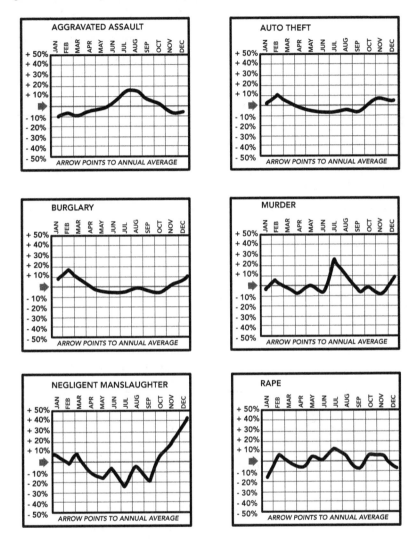

HEART DISEASE AND TWO OLD FRIENDS

In 1900, 20 percent of the total deaths in the United States were due to cardiovascular–renal diseases. Today, over 50 percent of our deaths are ascribed to heart disease. Of course, this proportion grows larger as we discover cures for many diseases that killed us fifty or sixty years ago, for it is fact that our overall death rate continues to decline nearly every year. Strangely enough, deaths from heart disease, at least in the northeastern United States, have had a cycle of 9⅔ years, and this cycle becomes somewhat frightening when it is placed on the same graph with the rise and fall in population of our old friends, the Canadian lynx, and the New Brunswick salmon (see Figure 15).

Fig. 15: Is This a Clue to Our Mystery?

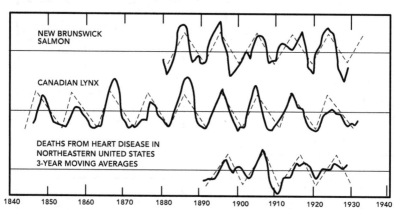

A similar 9.6-year cycle is evident in the abundance of Atlantic salmon, Canadian lynx, and human deaths from heart disease in northeastern United States (after Huntington).

What relationship could there possibly be between the cessation of our heartbeats and the abundance of lynx and salmon? Who can link these three events with reason and logic? Common sense disappears in the attempt. And yet, like the apple that fell at Newton's feet, the hint we see in Figure 15 is an invitation we cannot resist to carry our small light of inquiry deeper into nature's dark corners.

"What can be more foolish than to think that all this rare fabric of heaven and earth could come by chance, when all the skill of art is not able to make an oyster."

—Jeremy Taylor

7

The Rhythm
of Production

S EVERAL YEARS AGO the distinguished author Jim Bishop,
in a *Playboy* interview, called attention to the number of
coincidences in the lives and deaths of Abraham Lincoln and
John F. Kennedy.

At 7:30 A.M. on Friday, November 22, 1963, five hours before
he was shot in the back of the head, Mr. Kennedy told Kenneth
O'Donnell, his appointments secretary, that anyone who wanted
to exchange his life for the life of the President could do it. At
4:30 P.M., Friday, April 14, 1865, five hours and forty-five minutes
before he too was shot in the back of the head, Mr. Lincoln
said to his bodyguard, Major Crook, in reference to a possible
assassination, "I know of no one who could do it and escape alive.
But if it is to be done, it is impossible to prevent it."

In each case, as Bishop noted, death came on Friday; the assassin
was a political malcontent; the wound was in the back of the head;
the President's wife was at his side when it happened; and the
President was succeeded by a southerner named Johnson.

Lincoln and Kennedy were both elected President exactly fourteen years after having been elected to Congress; Booth shot Lincoln in a theater and Oswald was captured in a theater. Both assassins were shot to death before coming to trial. When Lincoln was buried, his son Robert moved to 3014 N. Street in Georgetown. When Kennedy was buried, his son John lived at 3014 N. Street in Georgetown. Both widows declined with thanks all invitations to the White House. Both widows could speak French.

Bishop also pointed out many more correspondences of a general nature such as courage, concern for the rights of the Negro, and such personal characteristics as wit. He says, "The parallels between the 16th President and the 35th run deep, beyond the credibility of the word *coincidence*."

His implication was obvious. The coincidences he had discovered, in his opinion, were more than *mere* coincidences. They had special significance or meaning.

If Jim Bishop is correct, the significance he implies is occult or mystical. It is neither statistical nor scientific.

What is the difference?

First of all, there is nothing wrong with coincidence from the scientific point of view. If you combine two parts of hydrogen and one part of oxygen, you get water. If you try this experiment again, you get the same result, a coincidence. A third try and you get water again, a second coincidence. After a sufficient number of coincidences, science will accept this behavior as the way things act.

What then are the differences between the coincidences that Bishop spoke of and those accepted by science? Basically there are two. First, science will accept as meaningful those coincidences that will enable you to predict. You can predict with complete accuracy that when you mix two parts of hydrogen with one part of oxygen you will get water. Second, science will accept as meaningful those coincidences that will lend themselves to statistical evaluation.

Bishop's coincidences do not enable you to predict. The fact that Lincoln and Kennedy were both followed by men of the same name did not enable us to say that Lyndon Johnson would be followed by a man named Grant. The fact, if it is a fact, that Eliza McCardle Johnson could speak German did not enable us to predict that Lady Bird Johnson would have this same skill. The fact that both Lincoln and Kennedy were shot between five and six hours after speaking of the ever-present possibility of assassination does not enable us to predict that any future President might experience a similar fate should he make a similar remark.

Nor can Bishop's coincidences be evaluated statistically, which, in fairness to him, was probably not his intent anyway. For to evaluate something statistically you need to know the number of non-coincidences as well as the coincidences so that you can compare one with the other.

For example, using imaginary facts, it may be that Kennedy had three buttons on his jacket while Lincoln had four; that Kennedy had eggs and bacon for breakfast, Lincoln, oatmeal; and that, on the morning of the fateful day, Kennedy showered while Lincoln merely sponged.

The point is that out of millions and millions of facts, known and unknown, the investigator selected only those that fitted into the picture he wanted to paint. We do not know how many instances existed where there was *no* correspondence between the two Presidents. Without such knowledge, statistical and scientific evaluation is impossible.

Now let us apply all of this to cycles.

We too deal with coincidences, but they are of the scientific kind, not the mystical or occult. They are scientific simply because they can be used as a basis for prediction and because they can be evaluated statistically. When cycles have repeated enough times with enough dominance and enough regularity we have a firm basis for making predictions.

A young man once asked his father, "How do we know the sun will come up tomorrow?"

His father answered, "Because it always has!"

How different this is from Bishop's coincidences.

If the young man's question had been slightly different, if he had asked, "How do we know the sun will shine at noon tomorrow?" the father, mindful of eclipses, might have answered that it *probably* would because it *almost* always did. Prior to the sixth century B.C., that is as far as he could have gone in his prediction. However, after the Babylonians learned to predict eclipses, he could have answered with assurance, one way or the other.

In modern economic cycle study, which we will begin to deal with in this chapter, we are about where the astronomers were before the Babylonians. We know about the cycles but we don't know, in advance, with *certainty*, when they are going to come early or late. Like the evening grosbeak on his biannual return to New England, we're not even sure if the cycle will appear at all every time that it is due. To know all this, in advance, is the next great step forward.

The second difference between our coincidences and Bishop's (our ability to predict, although admittedly only partially, being the first difference) is that we know, or can learn, all the coincidences that are *not* present in a series of figures we are examining, as well as those coincidences that *are* present. Thus we can measure the significance of the coincidences that interest us.

If every single fact of Kennedy's life, Lincoln's life, your life, my life, and a score of other lives could be recorded, there would doubtless be many coincidences shared by Kennedy with each of us. From the scientific point of view the question then would be, are the coincidences shared by Kennedy with Lincoln more numerous than the coincidences shared by Kennedy with any of the rest of us, or by each of us with each other? If so, are they more numerous *enough* to mean anything?

Obviously a comparison of this sort cannot be made in this case, but it is possible to do so in cycle study. To oversimplify the matter, you can find the best cycle (succession of coincidences?) in a real series of figures, for example, sugar prices. You can then randomize these figures, scramble them again and again, and look for the best cycle in each new series of figures you obtain. This will enable you to count how many scrambles it takes you to obtain, by chance alone, a cycle as good as the one you had discovered in the actual sugar prices with which you began. If it takes a hundred tries, you will know that your original sugar price cycle could not be the result of a chance arrangement of the figures more often than once in a hundred times. Thus it is a fairly strong assumption that the cycle you found in sugar prices is meaningful.

THE MYSTERIOUS PENDULUM OF PRODUCTION

It is fairly easy to accept the notion of cycles in plants, animals, and even human beings, for many of these are well known and accepted by biologists and physicians.

But when it comes to the matter of meaningful cycles in economic affairs, we touch a nerve that initiates unusual reaction and definite rejection from a large group, especially economists. One of this group, who was chief economist for one of our large corporations, stated the case for his fellow economists when he said, "If what you say is true, then all I have ever learned about economics is wrong, and my life's work is tumbled like a house of cards. I simply cannot afford to accept anything of the sort."

This gentleman also taught our young at one of our large universities. Perhaps his attitude is a microcosm of university teaching attitudes in general, a fact that our youth has been trying desperately to call to our attention.

I remember another remark from one company's executive vice president. "I believe you really have something," he said, "but I wouldn't want my people to know I took stock in anything like this or I'd never hear the end of it."

I was reminded of this gentleman's comments one evening when I read a thirteenth-century commentary about the compass in *A Short History of Science* by Sedgwick, Tyler, and Bigelow: "No master mariner dares to use it lest he should be suspected of being a magician; nor would the sailors venture to go to sea under the command of a man using an instrument which so much appeared to be under the influence of the powers below."

Cycles, in spite of those who have buried their heads in sand, do exist in economic affairs, and because of our country's concentration and worship of material things there are more statistics and data available to us in economics than in nearly any other area of study, although this is a small part of the whole field of cycles.

Let me proceed by showing you a representative sampling of cycles in the physical production of goods and services. These have been selected from the Foundation's monthly magazine, *Cycles*, which since 1950 has kept its members abreast of possible cycles in hundreds of phenomena ranging from war to the price of eggs.

My presentation may be somewhat unusual. Ten physical production cycles from various industries will be shown, but only as they appeared when they were published originally in *Cycles*. The graphs presented for your consideration are the graphs that accompanied each original article, some extending back to the early 1950's. No attempt has been made to bring these graphs and their cycles up to date. In most cases we had placed the cycle "on the table" for our members and then went on to other probings. My comments on each cycle will be excerpts from my comments accompanying the original article, for to include the full articles would fill nearly half this book.

Before we begin, let me anticipate one tantalizing thought that may have occurred to you. Am I not doing exactly what I gently chided Jim Bishop for doing in his Kennedy–Lincoln coincidences? By showing you just ten cycles in physical production, am I not marshaling those rhythms that will best prove my case while ignoring those that will not? No—for two reasons.

First, each cycle by itself presents evidence of rhythm that usually goes well beyond the area of mere chance, as you will see for yourself. Second, the ten cycles you will see represent only a microscopic portion of the cycles and alleged cycles from the Foundation's files at Pittsburgh. These few were selected because each has characteristics unique to itself, and they have been limited to ten so that our point can be made quickly and effectively. Many others will be placed "on the table" for your inspection as our investigation continues.

Now, as the auditors say, let's check the files.

THE SIX-YEAR CYCLE IN ORDERS RECEIVED BY GENERAL ELECTRIC

Cycles, September 1950: "For more than 50 years the orders received by the General Electric Company have fluctuated in a rhythm of about 6 years in length [see Figure 16]. Through wars and depressions, in spite of changes in management and changes in the nature of the business, the rhythm has persisted.

Fig. 16: The 6-Year Cycle in General Electric Orders Received,
1896–1946

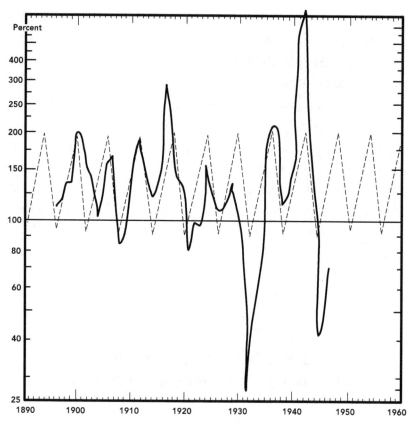

"... This rhythm has consisted of ten waves, clearly visible in the raw or unmanipulated figures.

"... A rhythm of this length is very common in American industry. Of thirty companies studied it is present in the sales and production of twenty-five. A rhythm of similar length is present, on the average, in each of six 100-year sections of tree-ring measurements; it has been alleged to be present in the alternate thickness and thinness of rock strata; it is present in barometric pressure in New York City and it is clearly present in sunspots with alternate cycles reversed.

"... This rhythm is significant because of the number and regularity of the waves. If it continues as in the past 57 years it is something well worth taking into account in trying to predict the future, not only of the General Electric Company, but of the country as a whole."

THE 5½-YEAR CYCLE IN AIRPLANE TRAFFIC

Cycles, December 1950: "Mr. Albert J. Kapteyn of East Hartford, Connecticut, a former airlines engineer at Pratt and Whitney, has called my attention to a 5½-year cycle in airplane traffic in the United States [see Figure 17].

"Airplane traffic is measured in billions of passenger miles. Figures are available from 1930 and are plotted as Curve A [remember all lines on graphs are called "curves" even if they are absolutely straight].... The tendency for growth to be more rapid at intervals of about 5½ years is evident by inspection.

"Curve B shows a 5-year geometric moving average trend of Curve A. The two values at each end are estimated. Curve C shows percentages above and below trend. Curve D is how a perfect 5½-year cycle (a periodicity) would look.

"... With a series as short as this we have had time for only about five repetitions of this cycle, not many on which to base judgment in regard to its significance. However, a 5½-year cycle is well established in other things. It was discovered in corn prices in 1875 and has been coming true ever since and cycles of about this length have also been found in European weather, cotton prices, pig iron prices, sunspot numbers, and the sales of at least two manufacturing companies.

"... By adjusting for the effect of this 5½-year cycle we can get a more accurate estimate of the fundamental underlying growth trend than we can get in any other way."

Fig. 17: The 5½-Year Cycle in Airplane Traffic, 1930–55

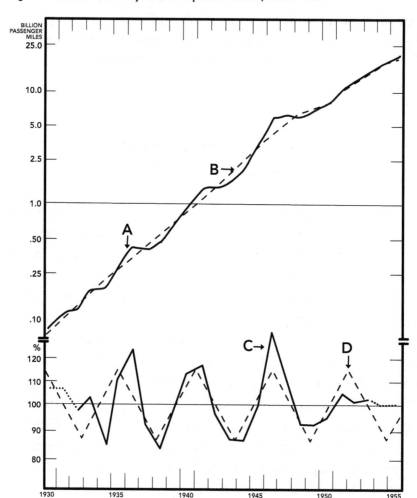

Upper portion shows growth (solid line) and trend (broken line). Lower portion shows amounts above or below trend and an obvious cycle approximately 5½ years in length. With so few repetitions there is no assurance that the cycle will continue; however, it cannot be ignored since a cycle of similar length has been discovered in many other phenomena.

THE 6.4-YEAR CYCLE IN ALUMINUM PRODUCTION

Cycles, January 1963: "The Foundation for the Study of Cycles has uncovered a 6.4-year rhythmic cycle in aluminum production [see Figure 18].... This rhythm has repeated twelve times during the 78 years that we, in the United States, have been producing aluminum. It characterizes and dominates the variations of this activity.

"... Growth is a characteristic of this industry. From 1885, when we produced less than 500 pounds, to 1962, production has increased eight million fold! Our interest in growth is because growth is the underlying structure around which the cycles oscillate. But our concern is primarily with the cycles.

"... The fluctuations recur with regularity [as you can see in Figure 18]. That is, they *tend* to conform to a perfectly regular pattern that can be fitted to them... in this instance, an ideal pattern that repeats regularly every 6.4 years.

Fig. 18: The 6.4-Year Rhythm in Aluminum Production, 1885–1962

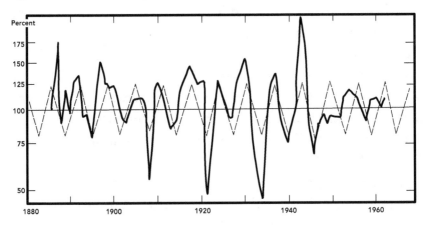

"A great many other things besides aluminum production are alleged to have rhythmic cycles of about 6.4 years in length. In the economic field we have a cycle of about this length in the liability of commercial and industrial failures, in the unit sales of General Motors passenger cars and trucks, in pig iron prices, in cotton prices, in rail stock prices.

"Are these cycles all one and the same? Only very accurate measurements will tell. If they are the same, is this mere happenstance, or is there some relationship?

"... At all events, with this strong and important rhythm in aluminum production, we have one more example of the almost universal presence of rhythm in the world around us."

THE 18⅓-YEAR CYCLE IN REAL ESTATE ACTIVITY

Cycles, February 1959: "Real estate activity in the United States has fluctuated since 1795 in a very regular cycle slightly over 18 years long. Whether the real estate people realize it or not, this cycle has been the basic fact of life in the real estate business. The graph [Figure 19] shows an ideal 18⅓-year cycle by means of a broken line and compares it to the actual Index of Real Estate Activity. The Index is expressed as a percent of normal with the 'normal' level of real estate activity as a horizontal line at 100 and the fluctuations shown above and below this line. This information is from Roy Wenzlick & Company who publish it regularly in *The Real Estate Trends*.

"... From 1795 through 1946 there were eight repetitions of the 18⅓-year cycle. The experience covers a time span of 150 years and the waves are too clear and regular to be denied or ignored. However, in view of the current picture, this cycle should be reviewed yearly and should not be relied upon until it is again clearly on the track."

Fig. 19: The 18⅓-Year Cycle in Real Estate Activity, 1795–1958

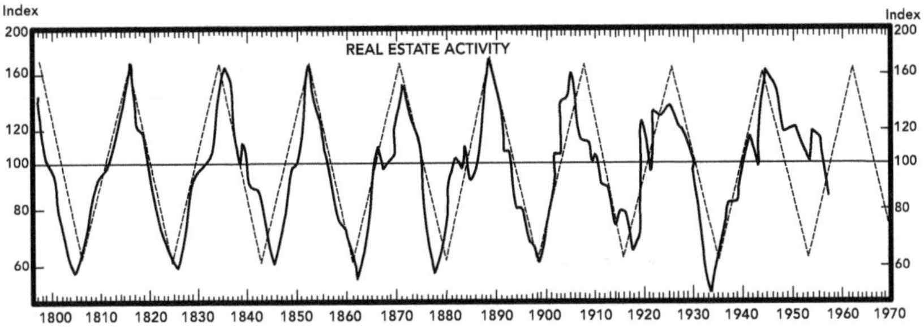

Data are for January of each year.

THE EIGHT-YEAR CYCLE IN CIGARETTE PRODUCTION

Cycles, April 1962: "From 1879 through 1958, cigarette production in the United States has been characterized by a rhythmic cycle with a wave length very close to 8 years in length [see Figure 20]. According to the test of significance developed by J. Bartels, this behavior could not be the result of chance more than 3 times out of 100. [Bartels, a German mathematician, developed a method of computing the odds of any cycle occurring by chance.]

Fig. 20: The 8-Year Cycle in Cigarette Production, 1879–1958

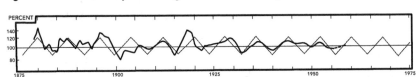

"In the actual data, this rhythm has usually expressed itself in changes in the rate of growth. Growth is first rapid, then less rapid. The reason for this rhythmic behavior is unknown.

"...8-year rhythms are present in many other phenomena and these other 8-year cycles tend to crest at more or less the same time. Could there be a common cause for some of these various behaviors?"

THE SIX-YEAR CYCLE IN STEEL PRODUCTION

Cycles, June–July 1955: "The production of steel ingots and castings from 1874 through 1947 has been characterized by a 6-year rhythm [see Figure 21]. This rhythm has repeated enough times and with enough regularity so that it cannot be the result of random forces.

Fig. 21: The 6-Year Cycle in Steel Production, 1874–1947 (Randoms Removed)

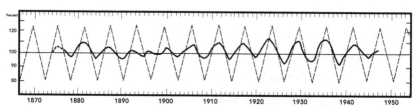

"... Steel production is rather complex and the 6-year cycle is only one of many tendencies. Note that the 6-year cycle tends to fade out in the period 1890–1905. It looks as if it might be starting to fade out, again. If so, we can expect, based on the 1890–1905 precedent, about three rather poor 6-year cycles after which the 6-year cycle can be expected to reassert itself.

"A cycle which gradually fades out and then reappears can be the result of the influences of another cycle, slightly longer or slightly shorter than the cycle which fades. I suspect that such a cycle is present in steel production. I shall investigate it and tell you more about it in another article. I shall also tell you about other cycles present in this series of figures. You need to know about several cycles before you are in a position to do any forecasting."

THE THIRTY-THREE-MONTH CYCLE IN RESIDENTIAL BUILDING CONSTRUCTION

Cycles, August 1956: "The 33-month cycle in residential building construction has continued for six and a half cycles since it was discovered by Cornell economists over 17 years ago.

"The chart [Figure 22] is in two sections. The left section is taken from *Farm Economics* of February, 1939. The right section is based on the F. W. Dodge Corporation's valuation of residential building construction contracts awarded in 37 states and has been drawn with a heavy line to indicate that the behavior unfolded *after* the discovery of the cycle.

"... Note the major distortion during the war period and the gradual return to normal after the war's close ... picking up the old rhythm again. Why?"

"The 33-month cycle is one of the best substantiated cycles in our files. There is no doubt in my mind as to its significance."

THE 9.6-YEAR CYCLE IN WHEAT ACREAGE

Cycles, May 1951: "We are happy to announce the discovery of a cycle of about 9.6 years in length which has been present in the acreage of wheat in the United States from the earliest figures, 1868, to the present [see Figure 23]. The recurrence of this cycle over the span of 85 years, and the strength and regularity displayed, made this cycle an important factor for agriculturalists involved in our great multi-million-dollar wheat industry.

Fig. 22: The 33-Month Cycle in Residential Building Construction, 1920–55

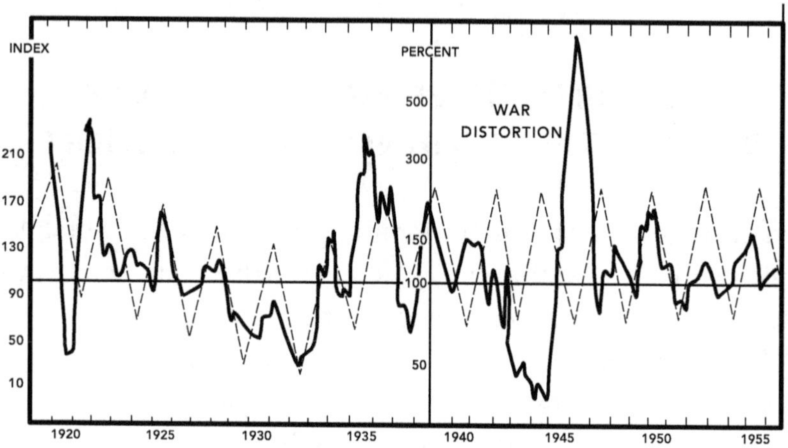

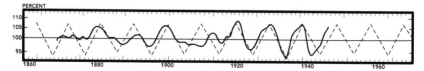

Solid line indicates percentage up or down from the same month of the previous year.

Fig. 23: The 9.6-Year Cycle in Wheat Acreage Harvested, 1868–1947

"As nearly as I can determine in a series of this length and regularity, the length of this cycle is 9.6 years. [Remember the Canadian lynx, and the salmon ... and the deaths from heart disease?]

"The pattern was badly distorted just prior to and during World War I, but with World War II there was no distortion."

THE 9.03-YEAR CYCLE IN
INSURANCE SALES

Cycles, March 1967: "Ordinary life insurance sales have risen consistently, year-by-year, since 1949. In 1965 sales totaled over $89 billion. [Since any professional insurance man refers to his sales as his "production," we bow to his categorization and include insurance sales in our sampling of cycles in economic production.]

Fig. 24: The 9-Year Cycle in Life Insurance Sales, 1858–1962

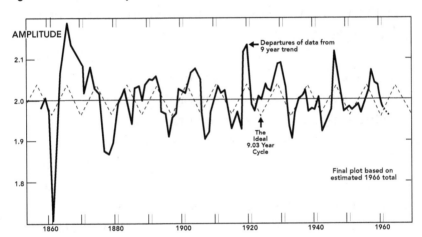

"A statistically significant 9.03-year cycle has been present in the sales record of ordinary life insurance since 1858, the first year of record [see Figure 24]. This cycle is not only statistically significant, which makes it important to cycle study, it is also prominent enough to exert an important effect on insurance sales which makes it important to the insurance industry."

THE 9.18-MONTH CYCLE IN TON-MILES OF THE CANADIAN PACIFIC RAILWAY

The Canadian Pacific Railway cycle was first announced in *Cycles* in a long article in its June 1951 edition. Rather than include many excerpts I will tell you the story, briefly.

Mr. G. Meredith Rountree was the Canadian Pacific Railway's chief statistician in the 1940's. In 1942 his company dispatched him to the Foundation for the Study of Cycles to make a study of the rhythmic fluctuations that might be present in their business. He worked at Foundation headquarters for approximately one year and his findings are a milestone in cycle research.

His work involved ton-miles, the number of tons of freight carried multiplied by the number of miles each ton is hauled. Like most railroads, the Canadian Pacific's freight business was somewhat seasonal. Mr. Rountree first removed the distortion of this seasonal business from his monthly figures, which were available back to 1903. The remaining data produced an unbelievable cycle that marched across his graph paper with *forty-nine repetitions* averaging 9.18 months per cycle (see Figure 25). This rhythm continued through World War I, stumbled twice between 1920 and 1925, picked up the cadence again until 1934, stumbled again, then corrected its step, and marched right up to World War II.

Fig. 25: The 9.18-Month Cycle in Ton-Miles, Canadian Pacific Railway, 1903–48

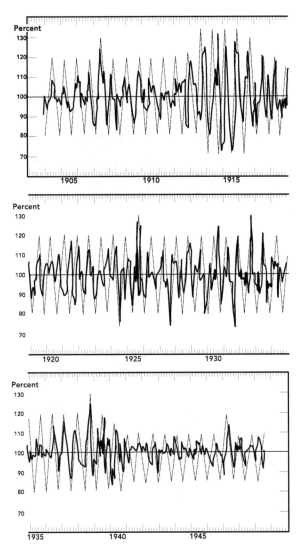

During World War II the cycle almost vanished, in contrast to World War I, but after the war it reasserted itself on the *same time schedule, same wavelength, and same calendar timing as before the war*! One cannot conceive of finding a pattern as regular as this, repeating so many times, in random numbers.

"*The door to the past is a strange door. It swings open and things pass through it, but they pass in one direction only. No man can return across that threshold, though he can look down still and see the green light waver in the water weeds.*"

—Loren Eiseley

8

The Cycle of Prices

EVERY TIME YOU make a major purchase you are, at least partially, trying to forecast the future price of that item.

Should you buy that new home now, or wait for real estate prices to go down? Of course, they might go up. Should you trade your automobile now, or will you get a better price deal in December? Corporations try to anticipate the moment when their new bond issue will bring the best possible price and housewives are always trying to outguess the supermarket manager.

Prices are affected by many forces, such as inflation, war, supply and demand, devaluation of currency, price controls, and changes in tariff laws. But underlying all these obvious and well-known causes is the mysterious and imposing force called rhythm.

Since World War II, prices have incessantly climbed to higher and higher plateaus, but even in their relentless upward movement they bob up and down in a behavior pattern that gives evidence of rhythm. They fluctuate, for the most part, in cycles, and this strange behavior seemingly has nothing to do with supply and demand, inflation, or any of the other well-known economic forces.

You cannot afford to ignore this inexplicable rhythmic behavior or you will be driving blindly through life. It is as if you were at the wheel of an automobile, driving backward at a speed of sixty miles per hour on a winding road with your accelerator stuck and your brakes out of order. To add to your predicament, you have no rearview mirror and you cannot turn your head to look at the road you are about to travel. All you can do is glance out of your side windows—and that's about all you can do when you look at today's prices.

In real life you can see what is happening *now* ... but you cannot see, even one minute ahead, what *will* happen. Moreover, you are always being propelled, irresistibly, at a constant speed of sixty minutes to the hour. You can't stop, you can't pause, you can't even slow down. And, like your suicidal automobile trip, if you don't guess right, you may be in for serious trouble.

Of course, in driving your automobile backward you might spot a clue or two which would help you decide the curves in the road. Perhaps to your right there are converging hills and to your left there is a stream running parallel to the road. Telephone poles might appear every so often, if you don't hit one of them.

In forecasting the future price of anything you have clues of this sort too, but the odds are still fifty–fifty that you will guess wrong. Ask any expert trader in the commodity and stock exchanges and he will quickly corroborate one fact that is so obvious that it is usually ignored—nearly every transaction involves one correct and one incorrect forecast of the future price of that item. Nearly every commodity price, every stock price, and anything else you care to name is either going up or down, perhaps in the next hour, the next day, the next week. Whenever a trade is made, one of the two parties involved, either the buyer or the seller, has guessed wrong about the future price of whatever was traded, despite all the facts and advice that are available.

But ... what if, while driving "blind" and backward, unable to see what is approaching, you suddenly realize that your road has a *pattern*? Wouldn't it be amazing if you discovered that it has *structure* and, insofar as this structure can be learned, the coming bends of the road are *predictable*?

Cycles have this structure, and although we still have much to learn, they can be used now to *help* us make forecasts. And regardless of how good or how practical the forecasts may be, the wondrous thing is that *from internal evidence alone* they can be made at all! We will improve our results as we learn more about our mystery and its cause.

Joseph, in biblical times, predicted a cycle of seven fat years followed by seven lean years, and the Pharaoh followed his advice to store up surplus food during the years of plenty so that there would be ample food during the years of shortage. After Joseph, the world waited several thousand years before another man was to come along and point out cycles in commodities and their prices. The Pharaoh listened to Joseph. The world has yet to heed the words of Samuel Benner. Joseph, presumably, had rare gifts of prophecy. Benner had only figures, graphs, and charts.

THE PROPHET FROM BAINBRIDGE

Samuel Turner Benner was born at Bloom Furnace, Ohio, in 1832. As a youth he worked in his father's iron works and after his Civil War service he married a senator's daughter, Ellen Salts, and became a prosperous hog and corn farmer in Bainbridge, Ohio.

In 1873 he suffered two setbacks over which he had no control. Hog cholera and the 1873 panic drove Sam Benner into bankruptcy. Penniless, he accepted help from his father-in-law, and with their only son, Stephen, the Benners moved to a farm in Dundas, Ohio, that had been placed in his wife's name.

Benner continued to farm, but now his mind was on other matters. He was determined to learn what caused panics, what caused the ups and downs in prices, and how to stay prosperous through good times and bad. In 1875, at the age of forty-three, he copyrighted his famous *Prophecies*, which were published under the title of *Benner's Prophecies of Future Ups and Downs in Prices*. Yearly thereafter he added postscripts and supplemental forecasts until 1907. He died in 1913 at the age of eighty-one, and someday history will proclaim him the father of cycle study in America, for he, like Leeuwenhoek with his microscope, opened up a completely new world of knowledge.

Leeuwenhoek's discovery of microbes did not benefit mankind until 200 years after his first observations. Hopefully the world is no longer on that same timetable, for we cannot afford to wait the 200 years until 2075 to convert Benner's discoveries of 1875 into a force for good. The world cannot continue to drive blindly for another century. Benner's major contributions to the knowledge of cycles were in the price fluctuations of pig iron and corn. He discovered a nine-year cycle in pig iron prices with high prices following a pattern of eight, nine, and ten years and then repeating, with lows following a pattern of nine, seven, and eleven years and then repeating (see Figure 26).

Fig. 26: Benner's 9-Year Cycle in Pig Iron Prices, 1834–1900

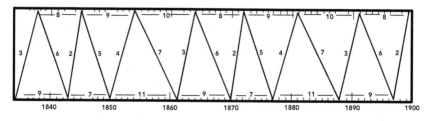

This chart is based on the work of Samuel Benner, first published in 1876. It was so accurate in forecasting the pig iron price cycle that it had a gain–loss ratio of 44 to 1 up to World War II.

Had you traded pig iron from 1875 to 1935 on the basis of Benner's cycle you would have made forty-four times as much as you lost.

Since 1939 Benner's forecast has not fared well. The true length of the cycle in pig iron prices, as we now know, is 9.2 years instead of nine years, and Benner admitted that he did not know how to deal with cycles of fractional length.

Gradually Benner's forecast got out of step with reality, but he never expected his original forecast, made in 1875, to hold true for more than twenty years. Were Benner still alive and issuing yearly supplements to his *Prophecies*, he probably would have learned all that was necessary to know about cycles of fractional length and would have adjusted later forecasts accordingly.

But we do not need to provide this great pioneer with any alibis. Benner's accurate forecast of pig iron prices for sixty years is the most notable forecast of prices in existence. He also discovered cycles in cotton, wheat, and pork prices, and a cycle in panics or depressions averaging eighteen years in length. I ask you to keep that length in mind as we explore our Foundation files for some other examples of cycles in various phenomena.

THE FIFTY-FOUR-YEAR CYCLE IN EUROPEAN WHEAT PRICES

Cycles, November 1962: "One of the reasons that people believe in the reality and significance of the 54-year cycle is the fact that Lord Beveridge discovered a cycle of this length in his famous periodogram analysis of European wheat prices, 1500 to 1869.

"… As so much of the belief in the significance of the 54-year cycle in all sorts of things depends upon this work of Lord Beveridge, I thought it desirable to examine his figures to see if there was a *rhythmic* cycle of this length actually present in his figures. I have done so. The result is shown [Figure 27]. Unquestionably, the figures *do* evidence a rhythm … the ups and downs do repeat time after time with a beat.

Fig. 27: The 54-Year Cycle in European Wheat Prices, 1513–1856

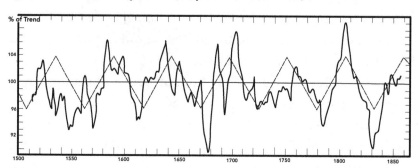

"… This does not mean that the crests and troughs come exactly 54 years from each other. The actual highs and lows are distorted, one way or another, by randoms and other cycles. There is, however, a *tendency* for *areas* of strength to follow each other at 50 to 60 year intervals and for such areas of strength to be separated by corresponding areas of weakness. As we look at the chart we see strength, weakness, strength, weakness, etc., repeated time after time across the page. Fifty-four years is the length of the perfectly regular cycle that most nearly fits these various successive waves.

"… The 54-year cycle discovered by Lord Beveridge therefore is not a statistical abstraction; it does refer to a physical reality. It is a reality in the United States, also.

"… Wheat prices in England are readily available from 1259. These longer series of figures have also been studied, and the 54-year cycle persists throughout . . . adding even more credence to the significance and the permanence of this important cycle."

Three months later I commented further about England's wheat price cycle:

Cycles, February 1963: "Of course, it is not surprising that from 1500 to 1869 English and European wheat prices behaved more or less the same way, but my recent work adds new elements to the picture. First, in England, the wheat prices from 1500 to 1869 really had rhythmic waves, something that Beveridge's work had not gone far enough to show. Second, I discovered that the waves had continued *forward* from 1869 to 1940 and *backward* from 1500 to 1260! Lastly, over this much longer span of time the length really did seem to hold up very close to 54 years.

"I hope you realize what a very stupendous thing it is that a rhythm should persist in a price series for over 700 years. The year 1260 is *very* long ago. It is a mere 200 years after the Norman Conquest; a full 200 years before the discovery of America; more than 400 years before the Industrial Revolution. Yet, over this long period of time . . . through wars, expansion, change from a feudal to a freehold agriculture and from a freehold agriculture to an industrial economy . . . the beat of 50 to 60 years has continued and has dominated!

"... A few years later, in 1949, studying some figures relative to the thickness and thinness of Arizona tree rings, I discovered that these figures, too, from 1100 to date, had what seemed to be a 54-year cycle. Here was something really important. If a natural science phenomenon like tree-ring widths has the same cycle as economic phenomena, we are on notice that we may be dealing with something much more fundamental than the mere ebb and flow of human price and production behavior."

In 1926 N. D. Kondratieff, Director of the Conjuncture Institute of Moscow, published a paper that announced that throughout the Western world economic phenomena went up and down more or less together in oscillations that had been, for the last two or three waves, about a half-century long. His work posed questions whose answers we are still seeking. Why do economic affairs fluctuate in rhythm? Why do economic affairs in all these divergent countries go up and down together? What is the cause?

THE 3½–3¾-YEAR CYCLE
IN CORN PRICES

Cycles, October 1955: "With a few minor exceptions corn prices in America are available from 1720 to the present. [Prices prior to the Revolutionary War were converted from British shillings for this cycle study.]

"… There are a powerful lot of months from January, 1720, to December, 1954, 2,820 to be exact.

"… Even the most casual study of a chart of corn prices, 1720 to date, shows evidence of a cycle a little less than four years long which repeats time after time with reasonable regularity."

This cycle has behaved in a unique manner since 1720, a behavior not calculated to make our job any easier. It changes its rhythm! After two 4¾-year waves it averaged 3⅔ years from top to top for twenty-five repetitions, until 1826. Then it shortened its beat to 3½ years for five repetitions. Then, just as suddenly, its length became 4½ years for four repetitions to 1860. From 1860 it has settled down to a regular 3½ years (see Figure 28) for twenty-five repetitions! Neither the early cycle of 3½ years, repeating for ninety-two years, nor the recent cycle of 3½ years, repeating for the past ninety-five years, behaved with such amazing regularity purely by chance. But what force caused the cadence to change?

Fig. 28: The 3½-Year Cycle in Corn Prices, 1860–1948

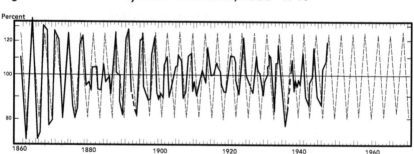

THE 17¾-YEAR CYCLE
IN COTTON PRICES

Cycles, January 1955: "Cotton prices for over 220 years have been characterized by a rhythmic cycle about 17¾ years in length [see Figure 29].

Fig. 29: The 17¾-Year Cycle in Cotton Prices, 1740–1945

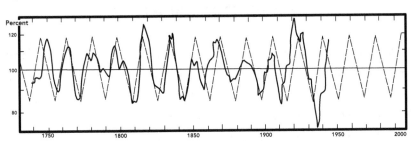

"... The typical cycle crests ideally in November, 1775, and every 17.75 years thereafter.

"... You must not think of this cycle (or any other cycle) in terms of its ideal crest. Think of it rather in terms of *areas* of strength and *areas* of weakness.

"... In the past we have had 21 tops and bottoms ... 15 came on time or within 2 years of perfect timing, 4 came 3 years one way or the other of perfect timing, 1 was 4 years off and 1 was 5 years off.

"... Let me remind you, again, that the 17¾-year cycle in cotton prices is only one of many cycles present in these figures. It's like the shortening in a pie crust, important as an *ingredient* in a forecast, but by itself it doesn't taste very good. If, however, you combine the 17¾-year cycle in cotton prices with the 5.91-year cycle in these figures, you can expect results better than by using either alone. If you add in more cycles, you could hope for an even better forecast."

I hope you took special note of the previous paragraph. It is included from the original 1955 article for a special reason. In it, and for the first time in this book, you are being put on notice that many phenomena have more than one cycle length and act as if they were influenced simultaneously by more than one cyclic force. We will return to this unsettling notion a little later.

THE 16⅔-YEAR CYCLE IN ENGLISH WROUGHT IRON PRICES

Cycles, May 1955 and July 1967: "Wrought iron prices in England, 1288 to 1908, clearly evidence a cycle about 16⅔ years in length [see Figure 30]. The figures cover a long enough period of time so that the cycle has repeated 38 times during 642 years.

"...When a rhythmic cycle persists in spite of changed environmental conditions we have additional evidence that it is of a non-chance nature.

"...Note that this cycle has remained a constant characteristic of these figures from before the Industrial Revolution, through the Industrial Revolution, and up into the era of modern technology.

"...Except for a few abnormalities scattered here and there over the 642-year period, the conformation to the perfectly regular pattern is quite astonishing."

THE 17¾-YEAR CYCLE IN PIG IRON PRICES

Cycles, April 1955: "Pig iron prices, 1784 to date, have been characterized by a rhythmic cycle about 17.7 years long [see Figure 31]. The span of time for which data are available (171 years) is enough for nine-and-a-half repetitions of the cycle.

"… Pig iron prices act as if they were influenced by a number of cyclic forces."

TWO STRANGE FACTS OF LIFE

Why are there different cycle lengths in different things? Why, for example, does the price of cotton have a 17¾-year cycle while corn prices fluctuate in a 3½-year rhythm?

The answer is simple. No one knows!

For that matter, no one knows why strawberries respond to red light waves, plums to blue light waves, and bananas to yellow light waves. All three colors of light are equally available but strawberries, plums, and bananas are selective. So are wheat prices, cotton prices, corn prices, and all the other phenomena that respond to cyclic forces. Most stock prices, as you will discover in the next chapter, fluctuate independently of one another, just as the various organs in your body have distinct and different rhythms. For now we can only accept this difference in cycle lengths as a fact of life just as we accept the sunrise and the sunset.

Fig. 30: The 16⅔-Year Cycle in English Wrought Iron Prices, 1288–1908

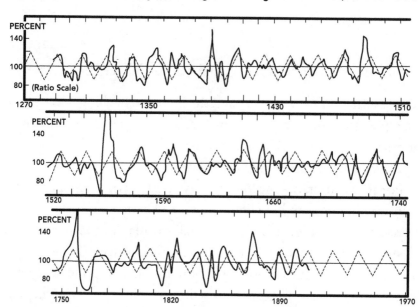

Study this chart carefully. You will note that although the cycle was distorted on more than one occasion the pattern always reasserted itself in step with previous behavior, an important clue that the cycle is much more likely to be non-chance or significant.

Fig. 31: The 17¾-Year Cycle in Pig Iron Prices, 1872–1950

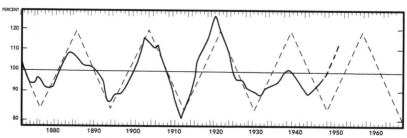

But there is another fact of cycle life that is even more perplexing. *Nearly every phenomenon seems to have more than one cycle, as if it were being influenced by a number of different forces, all acting on it at the same time.*

As you have learned, corn prices have a 3½-year cycle. But they also have a longer 5½-year fluctuation that was discovered long ago by Samuel Benner.

Cotton prices, you have just read, have a 17¾-year cycle. But they also have longer price cycles of fifty-four years and thirty-seven years and they have shorter cycles of 12.8 years, eleven years, 8.5 years and six years. There are possibly others, and it is this complexity of rhythms, all going up and down with different beats, that causes all but the stoutest hearts to abandon the search for the cause of cycles and go off in pursuit of something less difficult, like the fountain of youth or the lost continent of Atlantis.

And yet this concept will be easy for you to grasp when we consider weather as a perfect example of something with many cycles. Let's take the amount of rainfall at Anyplace, U.S.A. If we analyze the record of rainfall in this mythical city over a period of many years we will discover many cycles. The first of these is the yearly cycle. Some months have less rainfall than others and there is a normally dry season and a normally wet season.

Next, consider that some years *as a whole* are drier than others. If the dry years and wet years alternate we would also have a two-year cycle.

Now, the records of rainfall at Anyplace might indicate that, on the average, every other decade was drier than the one in between. This would give us a twenty-year cycle. And some centuries might be, on the average, drier than others—a 200-year cycle.

In our hypothetical case your dry periods from the one-year, two-year, twenty-year, and 200-year cycles will all coincide from time to time. There would be a dry month in a drier than normal year in a drier than normal decade in a drier than normal century. The opposite could also happen with all the wetter than normal periods coinciding.

Then there would be various mixtures of the wet and dry cycles. They might, at times, cancel each other out. At other times they might partially cancel each other out, and leave one or two cycles to dominate the scene. The situation would then become difficult to unravel with all the various cycles operating at the same time, reinforcing each other, canceling each other, and all mixed together in a seemingly unfathomable maze of ups and downs.

Yet this situation is not unfathomable. Once the different length cycles have been discovered and isolated, it is neither difficult nor complicated to combine them, through simple arithmetic, into a synthesis—one line representing the sum of all their different fluctuations and project this line into the future. Let's look at a fairly simple example from *Cycles*, September 1958, dealing with the price of oats.

In an earlier analysis, covering the price of No. 3 white oats at Chicago from January 1923 through May 1958, we had discovered a cycle of 26.64 months. An ideal cycle of this length is plotted in Figure 32 as A.

There is also a twelve-month seasonal cycle in oat prices. An ideal cycle of this length is plotted as B.

If we combine these two cycles, we have a curve (a line) that looks like C.

The general trend of oat prices during this period was downward, as you can see in D.

Fig. 32: The Price of Oats, 1950–59

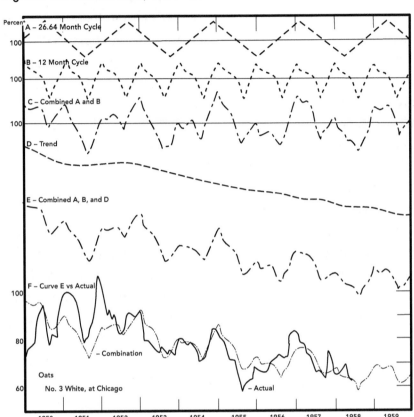

Note how two cycles in the prices of oats are combined with the trend, and compare this combination (dotted line) with the actual price (heavy line) in the bottom portion of chart.

When we combine this downward trend with A and B, we have a line that looks like E. Line E is reproduced again at the very bottom of the graph, and a heavy line of the *actual price* of oats from 1950 through April 1958 is superimposed on it. As you can see, by using only two cycles and the price trend line we did not come too far from the actual results. The variation between the two could have been caused by other unknown and still undiscovered cycles or randoms in the series of figures.

Our dotted line (E) was also extended through 1959 as a *forecast*, assuming that the two cycles would continue and that the price of oats would continue in its downward trend. Of course, either of these conditions could change. The downward trend of oat prices might reverse itself, or our two cycles could be overcome by a stronger cycle of some other length, still unknown. There could be many still undiscovered cycles in the price of oats. The government could also intrude to tamper with oat prices. War might affect the price. Thus if you were interested in oats, you would stick closely to your graphs, constantly making adjustments as Samuel Benner might have done with his yearly supplements.

This particular graph somewhat reminds me of Edison's early incandescent light. Many improvements and refinements will be made as our knowledge increases—but it does shed some light, dim though it may be, in the darkness. You can use the information even in its present far from absolute state provided you treat it only as a *probability* of what is to come, not as an absolute certainty.

All of us make use of *probabilities* every day. The weatherman says there is a 70 percent probability of showers, so we take our raincoat and umbrella. The probabilities are 8 to 5 that Notre Dame will defeat Michigan State, and so we wager on Notre Dame if we can get even money. The probabilities are that it will start getting cold in October, so we make certain that our furnace is checked and serviced in September. The probabilities are that next winter will be colder than last, so if you operate a natural gas company, you drill another well or two. The probabilities are that after 100,000 miles your car will begin giving you trouble, so you trade it in for a new one even though it is still running well.

Exactly the same sort of approach is required to make use of rhythm knowledge. This knowledge, incomplete as it still may be, can be invaluable when combined with business acumen and some common sense. The late General Charles Gates Dawes, former Vice President of the United States, former chairman of the board of the City National Bank and Trust Company of Chicago, and until his death a member of the board of directors of the Foundation for the Study of Cycles, once told me that he and his brother had made over a million dollars in the market solely as a result of his knowledge of cycles. He showed me brokerage statements that indicated more than this amount in clear profit.

Obviously he offered the best kind of proof that cycles can be a tremendously useful tool for the investor and businessman.

"You do have to know what time of market it is. Markets go in cycles like all the other rhythms of life."

—"Adam Smith," *The Money Game*

9

The Cycles of Wall Street

MANY SCIENTISTS ARE presently involved with cycles, and the number is growing each year. But for the most part each is studying cycles in his own particular field — economic cycles, earthquake cycles, cycles of disease, cycles of animal abundance, and many more. Few scholars, if any, outside of the Foundation for the Study of Cycles are studying cycles as such.

One reason for this state of affairs is that among those who have not examined the evidence there is a certain amount of skepticism about the meaningfulness of these cyclic behaviors.

To allay this skepticism I thought it would be helpful if our method and results were to be certified, as it were, by some of the world's leading statisticians.

This has been done, and I still think it was a good idea, although the concept was somewhat naive on my part. I believed that scientists would come flocking to the study of cycles once they were presented with irrefutable statistical proof that we were dealing with *facts*.

In the past few years two friends have argued that my idea was wrong. And what makes their comments particularly interesting is that they are the last persons in the world from whom one would expect advice of this sort. They are, of all things, statisticians themselves, and among the country's best, I might add.

They maintain that a fact without a theory to explain it, especially if it doesn't fit into the ordinary concepts of how things "ought" to behave, is merely a disturbing something to be ignored and, if possible, forgotten.

Independently both these men said, in effect, the same thing: "You have already made enough discoveries to convince any reasonable person that these mysterious behaviors do exist. It would be nice, of course, to prove by mathematics the soundness of all that you have done but don't let that be your prime concern. You are already at the place where you can say, 'These things are so.' Now go on from there and find out why!"

I do not mean to imply that my friends discount or decry statistical proof. They mean that all the statistical proof in the world, *by itself*, without some sort of theory or explanation, will not create the stir necessary to initiate full scientific participation in the study of cycles. A mere fact, by itself, makes no impact on the scientific community, especially if it runs counter to accepted ways of thinking. Were he alive and reading these words, Galileo would be nodding his head sadly.

All of this returns us to our search for the *cause* of our mystery.

Actually, however, we don't need to know cause to put a knowledge of cycles to practical use, as you have seen. We now have good and easy methods of detecting, isolating, evaluating, and projecting cycles.

We must, however, remember that cycles are not the whole answer. Cycles are distorted by randoms. Moreover, the cycles themselves occasionally "black out," miss a beat, give us two waves where there should be three, or evidence some other aberration before they get back on the track. Cycles, as yet, are not absolutely dependable, but they certainly help us to know the *probabilities.*

And nowhere is this more evident than in the stock market.

Not even the most ardent "cyclomaniac" would claim that all stock market fluctuations are the result of cyclic forces. Even if we knew all there was to know about cycles in the stock market, the most we could do would be to predict that part of the market behavior that was caused by cyclic forces.

But we can report facts that you should take into account if you are an investor, facts that you are not likely to learn from the hundreds of excellent books on the subject of stocks and bonds. I have, in my library, a volume that is generally acclaimed as the "investment bible" for anyone involved with the buying and selling of securities. I have no doubt that at least one copy can be found in nearly every investment broker's office in the country. Nowhere in its 700 pages of theory and practice is there a single mention of cycles *per se*! And yet, perverse, frustrating, unexplainable though cycles may be, you cannot ignore the fact that they exist if you are ever going to approximate the future probable behavior of the stock market.

Before his death General Dawes, mentioned briefly in the last chapter, asked me to inaugurate a service for banks and businessmen that would tell them what to expect regarding future activities of our economy. He suggested that I should charge a fair price for the service, that he would subscribe, that his bank would subscribe, and that he personally would write letters to all banks in the Midwest urging them to subscribe too.

Naturally, I was pleased and flattered by his tempting offer. However, I turned it down for the very simple reason that I did not feel I knew enough about cycles to be able to accept the money. Over two decades have passed since General Dawes made his proposal. If he were alive and were to make that same proposal today, I would still decline his offer, for despite all the clues we have uncovered in the past twenty years, our ignorance still outweighs our knowledge.

We have countless pieces that obviously belong to our "mosaic." They are real. But no one, yet, has been able to put them all together. No one, *yet*, has solved the great cycle mystery.

Perhaps this is the reason why the subject of cycles in the stock market is so carefully avoided in most investment literature. It cannot be substantiated scientifically, it cannot be catalogued, it cannot be categorized, and it does not complement any familiar investment theory. If it doesn't fit in anywhere, they say, let's leave it out, for it would only further complicate an already complicated subject. And furthermore, if cycles really do exist, why is there no scientific explanation for their cause? Thus goes their reasoning. How sad.

THE COMPLICATED BEAT

Stock prices, like most other phenomena, fluctuate in cycles. More exactly, like our complex cycle of rainfall in the previous chapter, stock prices act as if they were influenced by a number of *different* cyclic forces, all acting at the same time. Let me give you two more examples of this type of behavior.

The cardiograph record of your heartbeats shows a simple rhythm of perhaps seventy-eight beats a minute. But imagine what that chart would look like if you had a second heart that beat, let us say, forty-one times a minute. Now suppose you had three hearts, one beating seventy-eight times a minute, the second forty-one times a minute, and the third twenty-two times a minute. Can you imagine how erratic the chart of your heartbeats would be? And, of course, if you had ten or twenty or thirty hearts, each beating at its own special rate, you would have a mixture of ups and downs that would be impossible to unscramble unless you knew something about cycle analysis.

Or suppose we had a dozen or more moons, all of different masses and all revolving around the earth at different rates. Can you visualize how complicated our tides would be? Of course, knowing the laws of physics, we could work from cause to effect, and knowing the cycles of each of the moons by observation, we could trace their effect on the oceans.

But suppose our sky was perpetually overcast, like the sky of Venus, and we did not know the moons were there. It would be a long time, I am afraid, before it would occur to anyone that the seemingly haphazard movement of the water was due to anything but the winds. Patient work over many years might be necessary before the mystery could be unscrambled, the various moons postulated with certainty, and predictions made with accuracy.

Conditions similar to these prevail in the behavior of stock market prices. We know that there are cycles there, but they are fully as complicated as our pulse would be if we had a multitude of hearts, or as the tides would be with a multitude of moons. Consequently, I have lived for many years in a dilemma that is still unresolved. On the one hand, I have been reluctant to report about any *one* cycle in the stock market, just as a student of the tides in a world with many moons would hesitate to tell you about any *one* cycle in the levels of the waters. On the other hand, I still do not know enough to tell you about all the cycles. I knew even less in 1944 when I prepared a stock market forecast that received considerable attention.

MY FIRST STOCK MARKET FORECAST

Early in 1944, at the urging of a large brokerage firm in New York City, I prepared and delivered to them a forecast of stock market behavior. To complete this forecast I made a reconnaissance survey of possible medium- and long-term cycles in the stock market. The data used were annual averages of the Clement Burgess Index

1854–70 spliced to the Combined Index of the Standard and Poor's Corporation Index 1871–1943.

Only ten cycles over 4½ years in length were used in my projection, ranging from one of 4.89 years to one of twenty-one years. The forecast was as crude as Edison's first incandescent light. It employed only annual figures instead of daily, weekly, or monthly figures, which would have provided greater accuracy. No cycles less than 4½ years in length were included, although there are, without question, shorter cycles whose influence might have advanced or retarded the crests from the time indicated by the longer cycles. Also, since these stock figures go back only to 1854, those cycles of ten years or longer have had an opportunity to repeat only nine or less times, making their exact length difficult to pinpoint.

Anyway, this fool rushed in where men of good sense feared to tread, and the ten-year results can be seen in Figure 33. The ten cycles are synthesized into one forecast curve (broken line); the solid line shows what actually happened.

Fig. 33: A Stock Market Forecast

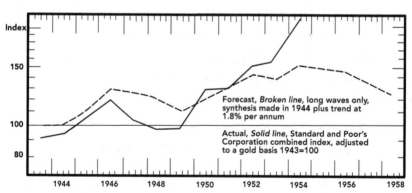

This forecast was prepared early in 1944 using figures through 1943 only. For the ten years during which the market behaved as predicted, the gain–loss ratio was 185 to 1.

The "forecast" correctly called for 1946 as the end of the bull market, correctly called for 1949 as the end of the bear market, and called for 1954 as the end of the bull market that followed. Over a ten-year period it had a gain–loss ratio of 185 to 1.

From the moment of its introduction everyone who came into contact with the forecast was warned by me that it was not to be considered as a forecast but merely as the result of a reconnaissance survey that had to be surrounded by the word *if*. It was merely a mockup to indicate *possible* future behavior *if* the indicated cycles were real and continued, *if* the length, shape, amplitude, and timing of the cycles had been correctly determined, *if* there were no other long-term waves that had not been taken into account, *if* the short-term waves less than 4½ years in length (which were not used) did not gang up on the long-term waves and distort them, and *if* no accidental factors entered into the situation.

After ten years the "forecast" went awry, but it is still a source of wonderment and pride to me that it continued to function accurately for a decade despite its primitive preparation. After all, Edison's first filament glowed only for a few hours.

Like the first light bulb, we have come a long way in our study of cycles since our first minor successes. The use of computers has greatly accelerated our progress at the Foundation during the past few years, but they have also shown the immense amount of work still ahead before we can forecast stock market activity successfully. In 1965, for example, an analysis of stock prices was undertaken with computers, searching for all possible hints of cycles in common stocks from 1837 up to that time.

When the search was completed and the computers had ceased to purr and the final logarithm table had been put away, we had discovered hints of *thirty-seven possible cycles in stock market prices*, ranging in length from 2½ years to nearly 111 years! Even the possibility of ten or twenty moons affecting our tides or ten or twenty hearts beating complex rhythms on our cardiograph chart seems fairly simple in comparison. To refine and verify all these cycles will take years. Eventually it will be accomplished, but while you are waiting, let me tell you some of the facts we already know about stock market behavior and forecasting.

FORECASTING BY MEANS OF CYCLES

First of all, let me explain *trend*. Trend is the general direction in which a series of figures is headed, up, down, sideways, etc. It changes its direction slowly. It is the element that represents growth, and in the stock market it accounts for the major part of all movement in the *annual* stock prices. Cycles and randoms play only a minor role.

Trend is that upward sweep you see when you chart your figures on a sheet of graph paper. Trend is the general direction your figures are going after the ups and downs and zigs and zags have been removed. It is usually plotted by averaging a number of years for each position on the graph. It is the erratic fluctuations of your figures refined to a single and fairly smooth line. In political terms, it is the "middle of the road" line between your various high and low points. This trend line can be projected into the future to show what the underlying growth element will be *if* growth behaves the same way in the future as it has in the past.

Growth, like almost everything else, obeys laws, and the law of growth is very simple; everything in the universe that grows will grow at a slower and slower *rate* as it grows older, and it will eventually level off and attain a stability from which it will die *unless something new is added to create a "rebirth."*

This little-known law can be applied to, among other things, any business operation. One man, who heads the largest organization of its kind in the world, credits what I wrote in an earlier book about the law of growth with helping him and his company to earn millions of dollars. New ideas, new products, new methods of distribution, and new personnel constantly keep his company alive and youthful, with no indication of leveling off after four decades of continuing growth.

The projection of a trend is a very tricky and complicated matter and its details will not be discussed here. What I want to point out, however, is that the upward sweep is a mixture of trend, cycles, and randoms. To know what the true trend has been you must remove the cycles and the randoms by some smoothing process. This smoothing process will remove the randoms and the shorter cycles. The longer cycles will usually remain but they must be determined as accurately as possible and accounted for in order to get a realistic projection into the future.

Let me give you an example. Suppose a certain series of figures has evidenced normal growth and, in addition, has a fifty-year cycle cresting in 1850, 1900, and 1950. That is, the cycle will be going up from 1875 to 1900 and from 1925 to 1950. It will be going down from 1850 to 1875, from 1900 to 1925, and from 1950 to 1975. The trend and the cycle are charted in Figure 34a.

When the cycle is in its upward phase (or leg), it will reinforce the trend and make it *seem* stronger. When the cycle is in its downward phase, it will tend to offset the trend and make it *seem* weaker.

But the trend, like the equator, is an imaginary line. You cannot see it when you look at your graph of actual price behavior. What you actually see, for the example given, is shown in Figure 34b. (In real life, of course, the line would have many more erratic zigzags than our simplified example, since it would be clouded by other cycles and by randoms.) It is from a study of this zigzag line that we must deduce (guess) the underlying trend.

Fig. 34: Trends and Cycles

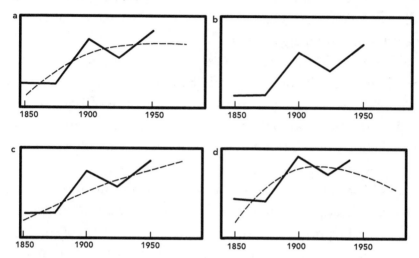

Now suppose we were not aware of a fifty-year cycle in our figures and tried, in 1950, to project our trend line into the future. We might guess that it would continue strongly upward as charted by the broken line in Figure 34c.

Suppose, however, we are doing our guessing in 1940 when the upward leg of the fifty-year cycle is only a little over half completed. If we did not know about the fifty-year cycle, our projection might well look like the dotted line in Figure 34d.

Obviously neither projection is correct. As we know by construction, the true trend line is the one shown by the broken line in Figure 34a, and we can only project this into the future when we take our fifty-year cycle into account. But herein lies the danger, for our fifty-year cycle has only repeated a very few times. It may not continue to come true. And if it doesn't, there goes your forecast.

Why wouldn't our fifty-year cycle continue to come true? Let's consider just two possibilities at this time. First, it has repeated only three times. As you know by now, this could have happened just by chance. Three times are not very many when you compare it with your playing cards alternating red and black through the entire deck, or the Canadian lynx and its abundance cycle.

But more important, and more germane to our stock market situation, the fifty-year cycle in our example could be a combination of many closely related cycles. A cycle of this sort is non-chance, it is perfectly real, it is statistically significant, and yet *it will not continue.* A study of Figure 35 will show you why.

Fig. 35: Three Cycles and Their Combination

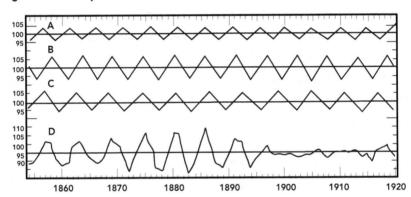

A is a 4.89-year cycle, B is a 5.50-year cycle, C is a 6.07-year cycle. D is how all three look when combined. A false cycle is created and eventually disappears.

For the moment look only at the bottom zigzag line (D). Note that from 1854 to 1896 we have what appears to be a fairly regular cycle that averages about 5.7 years in length. Then it disappears for about twenty years!

Our 5.7-year cycle *was never a cycle with a life and a beat of its own!* It was a combination of three other cycles, closely related. A is 4.89 years long, B is 5.50 years long, and C is 6.07 years long. While they marched along pretty much in step from 1884 through 1896, their combination produced a 5.7-year cycle. But by 1897 they were no longer synchronizing. For example, in 1896 C was going up while B was coming down. Everything flattened out and the 5.7-year cycle vanished. Around 1918 it is beginning to appear again as cycles A, B, and C begin to get back in step, but this is small consolation to your forecast made in 1896, isn't it? Furthermore, when it does reappear, the 5.7-year cycle will be upside-down compared to its previous rhythm. Its highs will be where its lows were before and vice versa.

HOW STOCKS BEHAVE

More than 1,600 stocks are listed for trading on the New York Stock Exchange, not to mention 1,200 bond issues. Stocks not only act with complete individuality, they also tend to group with others in their particular industry and behave differently from other groups, each group acting as if it had its own set of cycles.

Of course, many of the cycles are present in many different things, but they are present in different combinations and in different proportions, somewhat akin to words. We have only twenty-six letters in our alphabet but they combine into hundreds of thousands of words, all different.

To emphasize this difference Figure 36 demonstrates the varying behavior in fifty-six different groups of stocks over a three-month period. These charts represent the percentages by which each particular group was above or below the market trend as a whole, and are reproduced by permission of Mr. E. S. C. Coppock, of San Antonio, from part of his regular TRENDEX service to clients. Commodity prices, sales of individual companies, or almost anything else would show similar differences.

THE 9.2-YEAR CYCLE IN STOCK PRICES

There are those who insist that stock prices have no structure—that each day's motion is a purely random variation from the prices of the day before, triggered by tips and valid information flowing into the marketplace in a correspondingly random fashion.

Such people feel that a bull market is merely a period when, by chance, the upward movements predominate over the downward ones, while a bear market is a period of reverse behavior. According to them, stock prices evidence what is known as a "random walk" and any analysis of their past behavior is worthless in forecasting future behavior.

Of course, if stock behavior is an example of random walk, there can be no cycles except by chance. When one discovers a cycle that cannot be chance more than once in a hundred times or once in a thousand times, the proponents of the random-walk theory reply that "This is the hundredth time," or "This is the thousandth time." Were you to confront them with the cycle I am about to show you, they would have to say, "This is the five-thousandth time," for, according to the Bartels test of probability, the 9.2-year cycle *could not occur by chance more than once in 5,000 times.*

The 9.2-year cycle has repeated fourteen times since 1834, two years before the siege of the Alamo and ten years before Samuel Morse sent his first message over a telegraph line (see Figure 37). One evidence of a cycle's significance is the presence of cycles with the same period in other phenomena. Cycles variously measured from 9.15 to 9.25 years in length have been found in a variety of phenomena such as business failures, pig iron prices, partridge abundance, the levels of Lake Michigan, the thickness and thinness of tree rings, average wholesale prices, and the number of patents issued. Because so many other completely unrelated phenomena display similar cycles, we must seek the cause of our 9.2-year cycle outside the market itself.

Fig. 36: The Individuality of Stocks

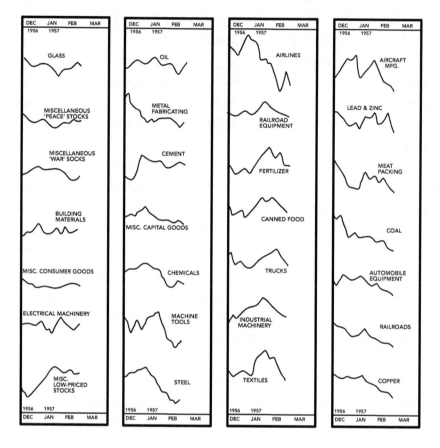

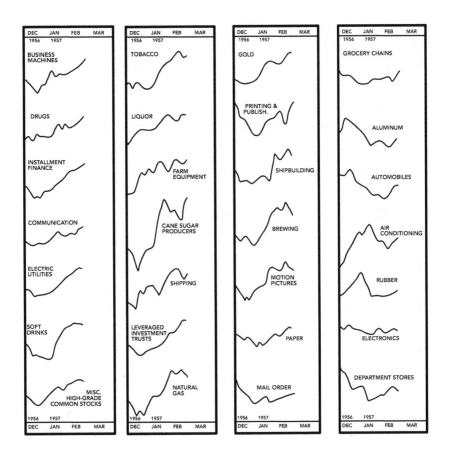

These charts emphasize the various behaviors of several groups of stocks. To further complicate matters similar variations are often found among stocks of each group (after Coppock).

What force triggers the 9.2-year cycle in these various phenomena and in stock market prices is still unknown.

Before we leave the 9.2-year cycle, I ask you to study Figure 37 once more. As you will note, its current ideal crest was due in 1965 (1965.4 to be exact). According to its past rhythm, it was scheduled to turn downward (below the trend) somewhere close to 1965.4. Remember, we are working with nine-year moving averages to compute our trend line so that we cannot actually know where our trend line is for 1966 until we have the stock averages for the nine years from 1962 through 1970. We will not know where our trend line is for 1967 until we have the stock averages for the nine years from 1963 through 1971, etc. And without our trend line, of course, we cannot tell whether the stock prices for that particular year were above or below the trend, nor can we compute, in percentages, how much above or below the trend line we were for any particular year as depicted in Figure 37.

Fig. 37: The 9.2-Year Cycle in Stock Prices, 1830–1966

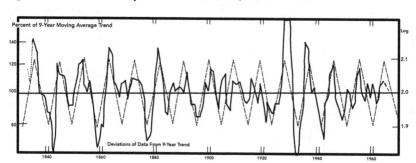

Thus as I write this, in the waning months of 1969, it is too early to tell if the 9.2-year cycle did, indeed, reach a crest in the vicinity of 1965.4 and then turned downward. However, I have completed some preliminary work that enables me to make an estimate of the trend for 1966 without waiting for the 1970 stock averages. Estimating where the trend will be, I have ventured to show the curve for 1965–66 as a broken line on Figure 37. You will note a peak in 1965, exactly at the time of ideal turning (1965.4).

Whether or not the 9.2-year cycle did hit its expected low in 1970 will not be known for several years (1966 through 1974 figures are required to complete the 1970 moving average trend). However, the prudent investor cannot ignore the behavior of what is perhaps the most important cycle discovered to date in stock market prices.

THE FORTY-ONE-MONTH CYCLE

Another cycle that has done all in its power to keep cycle scientists humble is one averaging 40.68 months in length. It has been present in industrial common stock prices since 1871 and was discovered in 1912 by a New York group of investors. These gentlemen had learned that the Rothschilds had analyzed British consols (government obligations) and had broken up the price fluctuations into a series of repeating curves that had been combined and used for forecasting.

The New York group hired a mathematician to discover the secret formula of the Rothschilds, and working with the Dow Jones Railroad Averages, he discovered a forty-one-month cycle, plus three others, which his employers used to help them invest in the market. Apparently they were very successful around World War I.

Some ten years after the original discovery, Professor W. L. Crum, of Harvard, noted a cycle of "39, 40, or 41 months" in monthly commercial paper rates in New York. Almost simultaneously, Professor Joseph Kitchin, also of Harvard, discovered a cycle that he called forty months in six economic time series, bank clearings, commodity prices, and interest rates in both Great Britain and the United States from 1890 to 1922.

As far as I know, it was not until 1935, twenty-three years after the original discovery, that this cycle was again noticed in the stock market. Our old friend Chapin Hoskins, who knew nothing of the earlier work, discovered this cycle in many series of price and production figures, including common stock prices. Early in 1938 he made an extensive study of this cycle for one of the large investment trust services.

Figure 38 shows the forty-one-month cycle (now refined to 40.68 months) from 1868 through 1945. As you can see, while its waves are not identical to an ideal 40.68 wave, which is represented by the broken zigzag, there is an amazing correspondence between them. This cycle persisted through wars and peace, good times and depressions.

Then, in 1946, something strange happened to our cycle. Almost as if some giant hand had reached down and pushed it, the cycle stumbled, and by the time it had regained its equilibrium it was marching completely out of step from the ideal cadence it had maintained for so many years. As you can see in Figure 39, it has regained the approximate beat of forty-one months or so, as before, but its behavior now appears upside-down on our graph.

Scores of explanations and reams of paper have been expended to explain this behavior. We are familiar with most of the possibilities, such as distortion by random behavior, two or more other cycles of near lengths, and even a general public knowledge of this particular cycle, which may have had a distorting effect on its timing. But, in truth, no one can positively explain what happened in 1946 any more than they can explain the regularity of the rhythm for all the years that preceded it.

THE ENDLESS PARADE

If you were to review all the old issues of *Cycles*, you might find as many as two hundred different cycles alleged in stock prices. It would be an easy matter to fill this book with descriptions of various stock market cycles to which we attach some significance. Chapter upon chapter could be filled with "coincidences"; for example, the 18.2-year cycle in the stock market matches cycles of similar length in marriages, thickness and thinness of Java tree rings, floods on the Nile, immigration, real estate activity, loans and discounts, construction, and panics.

We could tell you about the 6.01-year cycle and the 17.16-week cycle and all of the thirty-seven hints of cycles recently discovered by our computers. To refine and verify these thirty-seven possible cycles in the stock market, as I mentioned earlier, will take years. Yet when this is finally completed and the cycles that stand up are combined and projected into the future, we still have little assurance that our forecast of future price behavior in the stock market will come true for very long. What good are cycles, then? For forecasting! But only when we know much more about them than we do now.

Fig. 38: The 41-Month Rhythm in Stock Prices, 1868–1945

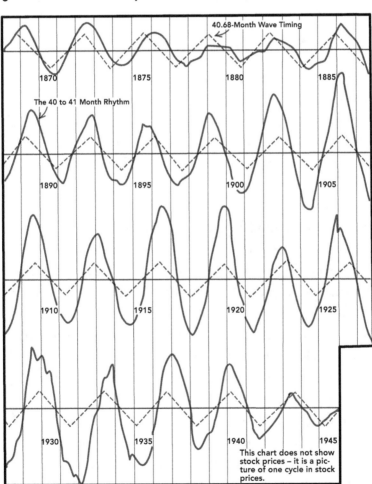

Fig. 39: The 41-Month Rhythm, upside-down, 1946–57

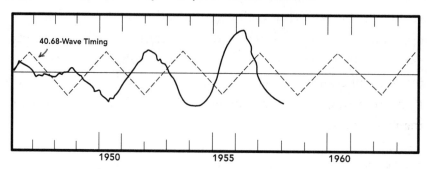

A REPLY TO ROGER BABSON

Many years ago I received a letter from one of America's great geniuses in the field of investment, Roger Babson. Mr. Babson, too, was searching for the answer to the stock market cycle enigma. His letter, and my reply, will perhaps give you some concept of the mystery that confronts man in the market. He wrote:

Dear Mr. Dewey:

Perhaps some month you would write an article on the causes of cycles—taking the business cycle as an illustration. The Babson Organization is coming to believe that the *impatience* of people to buy or to sell is surely the cause of the Stock Market Cycle.

Would you say it is also an important cause of the general business cycle? We are now getting data on the "feelings" of over 400 different communities, but we have not yet determined how to weigh these.

How do you feel about new inventions, products, and methods which are now on drawing boards and in test tubes affecting the duration of a business cycle? Surely the automobile industry has been a factor almost equal to a world war. If atomic energy is used for peaceable purposes could this be a factor in lengthening the normal business cycle? You will be interested to know that we have on our payroll three persons who spend their entire days at the Patent Office carefully scrutinizing all the patent assignments.

I replied to Mr. Babson as follows:

Dear Mr. Babson:

Answering your last question, first, I believe that inventions are important elements in the *growth trend* of individual companies, of individual industries, and doubtless of manufacturing as a whole, but I do not believe they have *any effect whatsoever* upon the duration of a business cycle.

As I see it, business cycles are generated by consumers.

I am not sure whether it is the *feelings* of people as consumers or the *energy* of people as consumers which cause business cycles. Perhaps it is both, but my guess is that people's feelings are probably the most important factor.

I think you are on the right track in attempting to measure *feelings* of various communities.

If I were given the job of measuring the feelings of a community, I would keep as far away as possible from bankers, executives, and intellectuals. Such people are not close to feelings of the mass as bartenders, barbers, taxicab drivers, laborers, garage mechanics, waiters, and other average folk. Bankers and executives will tell you what they *think*, but this isn't what you want to know. You want to know what the great body of people *feel*.

I dare say that in attempting to determine the feelings of communities you have proceeded just as I would have done.

It seems to me—as it doubtless does to you—that impatience is one aspect of *feeling*. I can imagine that it could easily be of great importance.

I once believed that stock prices were determined by the mass emotions of the buyers and sellers of stock. I felt that when stock buyers were optimistic they bought, when they were pessimistic they sold. This may indeed be a factor in market prices, but I no longer believe that it is the controlling factor. My present conjectures are something like this:

Consumers of shirts, let us say, suddenly feel pessimistic and fearful. They refrain from buying shirts. Presently, shirt retailers note large inventories and refrain from buying. Shirt wholesalers soon cut back on their order to manufacturers. Eventually manufacturers of shirts are forced to curtail production. Very smart stock market operators, learning of the actual or proposed curtailment of production, sell the stock of the shirt manufacturer.

As shirt manufacturing acts as if it were influenced by rhythmic forces of precise mathematical length, we must conclude—if the above conjectures are correct—that something stimulates the buyers of shirts at precise mathematical intervals. As they act together more than not we can conclude that this *something* is environmental—that is, outside the individual shirt consumer. What this environmental factor is, is not known.

The production of shirts does not fluctuate in any simple way. It acts as if it were subjected simultaneously to random factors and to a great variety of rhythmic forces which sometimes pull together and strengthen each other; sometimes oppose and weaken each other. If shirt manufacturing is the result of shirt consumption, it follows that the consumers of shirts are, on their part, influenced by a variety of cyclic forces, and because consumers act the same way more often than not, we may conclude that all these cyclic forces are environmental.

So far, it is clear sailing. Just as we are bathed by light

of various wave lengths to which our eyes respond, I think it perfectly reasonable to assume that we may be bathed continuously by energy waves of much greater wave length which we perceive dimly through our emotions—waves which alternately elate and depress us and/or energize and relax us.

But here is where the theory breaks down—or perhaps we should say where it has not yet been built up. Why is it, if all this is the case, that buyers of cigarettes, for example, respond predominantly to 8-year environmental cycles, whereas buyers of shirts respond more actively to 2-year cycles? What differentiates the buyer of cigarettes from the buyer of shirts, *especially when he is likely to be the same person*? This seems utterly fantastic and unreasonable to me, but it seems equally unreasonable to assume that the manufacturers of shirts, for example, have very much to do with the demand for shirts. The cycles *must*, pretty largely, originate in the consumer.

Perhaps someday we will understand all these things better. But, in the meantime, if we want to forecast the behavior of any figures which act as if they were influenced by these cyclic forces, we can be assisted if we learn all the wavelengths involved as reflected in the figures themselves. This is true even if we do not yet know the mechanisms whereby the cyclic forces operate.

THE BLANK SPOT ON THE MAP

Forecasting the stock market is, ideally, a full-time occupation. At the very least it is a full-time avocation. For the person who is willing to give the subject the proper amount of time, a knowledge of cycles can be of real help, as I know from correspondence and meetings with many members of the Foundation.

The failure of economics to become a science is due to the failure of economists to recognize that there are natural rhythmic forces in our environment to which human beings respond. It will never become a science until economists learn to distinguish between the effects of these forces and the true economic forces also present.

Forecasting economic events involves forecasting three separate elements or factors. First, you must forecast the basic underlying growth trend, the situation that changes only slowly over the years.

Next, you must forecast the cyclic factor, the rhythmic ups and downs that, if you have determined them correctly and if they are significant, usually continue.

Lastly, you must forecast the noncyclic factors. As part of this third element, when you are forecasting prices, or anything measured in dollars, you must take into account the fact of inflation and remember that it now takes two or more paper dollars to buy what could be bought for one gold dollar, if by luck you had one.

I know little more about the noncyclic elements in the stock market than you do. Probably not as much. And I have always rejected the temptation to allow myself to be drawn into giving my own opinions on subjects about which I know nothing. You can get opinions from countless other sources of information.

But the trouble with most sources of economic information is that they probably know little or nothing about the rhythmic cycles, and their lack of knowledge leads them to make false deductions about cause and effect. For example, a bit of bad war news hits the front page and the price of stocks goes down. "Ah ha," the experts say. "Bad war news means lower stock prices!" But suppose the decline was really due to the downturn of a cycle and the dip in the market had nothing to do with the bad war news?

However, with their bad war-news theory, many would be led to make a false forecast the next time bad war news appeared. The next time, after bad war news appeared and the experts predicted a decline, the price of stocks might go up! That's why forecasters have ulcers.

It is impossible to make adequate economic forecasts without taking cycles into account. In fact, it is impossible to have an adequate economic theory without taking cycles into account. Economics is properly the science of the *divergence* from cyclic patterns. It is as ridiculous to attribute the nine-year cycle to, let us say, *economic* factors as it would be to say that *economic* factors are responsible for the summer boom in the ice cream business or the winter boom in fuel oil.

A knowledge of cycles can be as valuable in your forecasts of stock market behavior as a barometer is to a weatherman, but you must never forget that the barometer is only one of the tools used to prepare a weather forecast.

Nevertheless, who would think of preparing a weather forecast without a barometer? I know a professional stock market forecaster who uses *nine* different methods to show him what's ahead. This is the sort of thing you should do if you want to be a forecaster.

The forecaster I refer to won't use a method until he has tested it carefully and painstakingly for at least *ten years*. He does not use a knowledge of cycles because he has been testing cycles for only about seven years. Some time ago I wrote him to inquire how his cycle tests were coming out. As nearly as I can remember his words, he replied that the results were phenomenal and amazing. I have no doubt that if his present success continues, he will, in time, commence to use a knowledge of cycles as a tenth method to help him forecast market behavior.

Through the years I have had to answer the same question an uncounted number of times. It goes something like this: "Why don't you concentrate all your time and effort on the stock market cycles?"

My reply usually raises a few cynical eyebrows. I say, "Because, basically, it isn't my job. My job is to find out about cycles—all sorts of cycles—how they work, what causes them, how to tell significant ones from random ones . . . all that sort of thing."

To learn one thing I may have to study corn prices; to learn another I may have to study war; to learn another I may have to study earthquakes. The subject is as big as the whole wide world. If I limit myself to one little corner of it, I'll never get anywhere.

So my choice is simple. Shall I become a stock market expert, or shall I try to learn something about cycles? I cannot do both, and since I am not worried about the source of my next meal—and what more does one really need?—I can, fortunately, make a choice.

I'm trying to learn all I can about cycles ... one of the great blank spots still remaining on the map of science.

"They say it is observed in the Low Countries (I know not in what part) that every five and thirty years the same kind and suit of weather comes about again... ; they call it Prime... computing backwards, I have found some concurrence."

—Francis Bacon

10

Why Does it Rain on January 23?

I T HAS BEEN said that the mark of an educated man is his resistance to new ideas. This characterization is not made disparagingly. The educated man knows so much that he knows why a new idea won't work. You'll never hear him say, "Why don't they try it?" or "Why don't they do it this way?" These questions are usually asked by people who would not ask if they knew more.

But sometimes educated people know too much. I recall a story from World War I. The German zeppelins were striking terror in the hearts of the people of London, and the British bullets, instead of destroying them, were going right through the tough airship skins. What was needed was a bullet that would ignite on contact with the balloons, and British scientists applied various explosives to the bullets to achieve the desired results. Every attempt produced failure.

One day an old man came to the war office and said he had the solution. He told the harried military experts to put a dab of dynamite on the nose of their bullets. The dynamite, he said, would ignite the silk covers of the balloons.

Of course, no one paid any attention to him; everyone knew that dynamite is relatively nonexplosive. It was unthinkable that it would explode upon contact with silk. But the old man persisted. Finally, to end their annoyance, one of the experts went with the old man to his back yard. The test was made. A bullet with dynamite on it, fired through a piece of silk, *did* set the fabric on fire.

The answer was simple. Dynamite is nitroglycerine and a filler. In the process of being fired, the filler fell back and left a few drops of pure nitroglycerine on the bullet's nose. When this hit the taut silk it exploded.

The problem was solved—in spite of the educated men at the war office. In this case they knew too much.

Something of the sort may be happening with regard to using cycle knowledge as an aid to weather forecasting. Although largely ignored by many, the possibility of cycles in weather has occupied the attention of some of the most eminent meteorologists, who have felt that long-range weather prediction is possible only through an understanding and application of cycles.

BROADWAY AND THE BAROMETER

Whether you call it atmosphere or just plain air, there are approximately 5 quadrillion tons of the stuff clinging to our earth. Here, on the surface, we're at the bottom of the pile and the air pressure at sea level is about 14.7 pounds per square inch, or one ton per square foot.

Air pressure is measured by a barometer and recorded as inches of mercury; 29.91 inches of mercury equals 14.7 pounds per square inch, and so on, up and down the scale. Usually a falling barometer indicates that a storm is coming and a rising barometer that good weather is on the way.

Since 1873 barometric pressure at New York City has moved in a cyclic pattern that has averaged 7.6 years. The precision with which this strange cycle has repeated can be seen in Figure 40. The actual barometric pressure has been smoothed by a three-year moving average, shown by the solid line.

Fig. 40: The 7.6-Year Cycle in New York's Barometric Pressure, 1874–1967

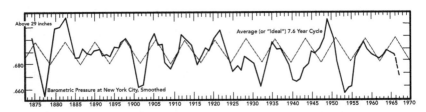

Significantly, of the twenty-four turning points shown in the chart, a total of twelve came within half a year of ideal timing and in only one instance was a turning point more than two years from the ideal. A Bartels test of significance was performed in order to rate the behavior of this cycle better. This test showed that such a performance could have resulted by chance *no more than one time in forty-eight.* Adding to its credibility is the fact that the cycle continued to perform in the ideal pattern after it was discovered in 1953; in fact, its behavior has been dramatically precise through 1968.

What does it all mean, you may ask. Why do we study repetitive behavior in barometric pressure at New York City? These are logical questions. First, there is the most obvious answer—we study it because it is there. Secondly, such work may be invaluable in future long-range forecasts. A third reason is that it may be possible that this cycle found in nature may tend to influence other things in seemingly unrelated areas.

For example, cycles of this length have been found in other natural science series. Douglass and Abbot both reported cycles of this length in tree ring growth; Alter and Lane both found similar lengths as minor cycles in the behavior of sunspots; Abbot discovered a 7.58-year cycle in solar radiation and one of 7.66 years in the average mean temperature in Berlin. Another barometric pressure study was performed by Clayton, who found a 7.54-year cycle at five widely separated weather stations throughout the world.

Also, cycles of this approximate length have been reported in pig iron prices, steel prices, stock prices, sales of a public utility company, and revenue freight ton-miles.

Could it be that changes in pressure influence man, and man, in turn, reflects this influence in many ways? Long lists of reactions to a falling barometer in both animals and humans have been compiled. Generally the symptoms are restlessness, irritability, an increase in traffic and industrial accidents, forgetfulness, and sleeplessness.

One study by two biostatisticians, Digon and Bock, of the Pennsylvania Department of Health, shows that suicides tend to increase dramatically whenever barometric pressure changes by 0.35 inches or more, and there was also some indication that a falling barometer was more dangerous than a rising one. The two scientists did not offer any possible explanation for the apparent fact that changes in barometric pressure may trigger acts of self-destructive violence.

Whether or not there is any cause-and-effect relationship between the barometric pressure cycle and any psychological or economic behavior will require long periods of extensive observations at various latitudes. But what a fascinating subject for someone to pursue! Does barometric pressure at places other than New York City have a 7.6-year cycle? Is the behavior worldwide? As the amount of air surrounding our planet is fixed, one would imagine that a 7.6-year cycle in pressure in one part of the world would have to be offset by an upside-down 7.6-year cycle in some other part of the world. Is there such an upside-down 7.6-year cycle, and if so, where? Also, in these other parts of the world do economic affairs also have an upside-down 7.6-year cycle? No one knows, but it is extremely important to find out if we are to understand the rhythmic forces to which we as human beings are subject.

THE RHYTHM OF THE RAIN

The weatherman and his public image have shown great progress since 1870 when the U.S. Signal Corps initiated our first national weather service. Each evening as we watch our favorite television prognosticator give his or her odds on rain occurring in the next five days it is difficult to realize that until the late Henry Wallace was Secretary of Agriculture (1933–40) there were no government forecasts made for more than twenty-four hours into the future.

Concerned with the obvious effect of weather on crops, Wallace suggested that the Weather Bureau attempt forty-eight-hour forecasts. Now, with advanced computers, radar, and the Tiros satellites monitoring the move of every cloud formation, it is possible to make fairly accurate general weather predictions almost two weeks in advance—and when meteorologists accept Einstein's famous premise that "God does not play dice with the universe" and recognize that there are rhythmic behavior patterns in climatology, they may be able to predict weather several years into the future!

Yet many of them continue to work with their heads in the sand—or the clouds. Show them the following graph (Figure 41), and they will tell you that the obvious 4.33-year cycle in Philadelphia precipitation since 1820 is mere coincidence.

This cycle, if real, is a small factor in total precipitation, probably accounting for only slightly more than a one-inch change in a year. Yet if the cycle is significant, if it is one of the reasons for changes in levels of precipitation, then it is another important clue to helping us unravel our puzzle.

Fig. 41: The 4.33-Year Cycle in Philadelphia's Precipitation, 1820–1960

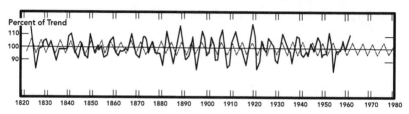

As a further check on our Philadelphia figures the precipitation figures from nearby New York City and Baltimore were both investigated. Each produced the same 4.33-year cycle. Of the three cities the Baltimore cycle is most pronounced (Figure 42). This cycle could occur by chance only once in 400 times.

Fig. 42: The 4.33-Year Cycle in Baltimore's Precipitation, 1820–1960

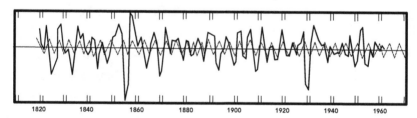

WHY DOES IT RAIN ON JANUARY 23?

A heavy rainfall usually descends on Brisbane, Australia, on January 23. Dr. E. G. Bowen, Chief of the Radiophysics Division of the Commonwealth Scientific and Industrial Research Organization in Australia, reported that on certain days, such as January 23, it rained in Brisbane and that this has occurred so often that it could hardly be chance.

Later the U.S. Weather Bureau corroborated Dr. Bowen's findings concerning a recurring pattern of high and low rainfall on the same calendar days. Dr. Bowen suggested that since certain meteoric showers recur at regular dates, the entrance of meteoric dust into the earth's atmosphere may have been the culprit, but there is still no proof as to the exact cause of this yearly shower.

THE 100-YEAR CYCLE

The late Professor Raymond H. Wheeler, while at the University of Kansas, engaged in an immense project to summarize, in an organized fashion, all of recorded history. The compilation of the 2,500 years of records from which Wheeler derived so many brilliant hypotheses took 20 years and at one time occupied as many as 200 people. You will meet him again when we consider the cycles in war.

As Wheeler's work progressed, he noticed a marked correspondence between the historical record of human events and the weather at the time the events occurred. Wheeler's chief interest was in the relation and reaction of man to his environment and, of course, weather and climate are a major element in our environment.

Professor Wheeler discovered many cycles during the course of his work but he felt the most important one to be a climate cycle of about 100 years' duration. To this 100-year cycle of weather change he tied the record of human events and concluded that the two factors, weather and human events, were intimately related.

Wheeler's 100-year cycle is divided into four phases (see Figure 43).

Fig. 43: Wheeler's Phases in Climate

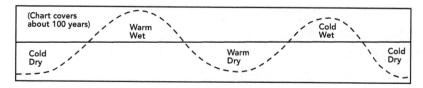

This cycle averages 100 years, although it may run as short as seventy years and as long as 120 years. Also, the four phases are not precisely equal in duration. In general, the cycle has a warm and a cold phase, with each of these having a wet and a dry period. These expressions are only intended to describe world conditions in general and not the weather conditions for specific geographic locations at specific times.

Wheeler noted that the general character of the climate over a period of years can be seen in historical cycles. Because people are certainly affected by the character of the weather, similar events have occurred throughout history during the same phases of the 100-year climate cycle.

COLD-DRY

The cold-dry period, according to Wheeler, is a time of general individualism, with weak governments, migrations, and other mob actions such as race riots. Class struggles and civil wars ranging from palace intrigues to revolutions occur during the general anarchy of the cold-dry period. People are cosmopolitan and Epicurean, borrowing culture and living by superficial and skeptical philosophies. (In 1949 Wheeler indicated that we were passing through a cold-wet period and heading into this ugly cold-dry era. Draw your own conclusions.)

As this phase nears an end and fades into the next phase, leadership emerges and societies become stabilized; new governments develop and nationalistic spirit revives. Wars take the form of expansion and imperialism.

In the transition from the cold to the warm era, human energies operate at a high level (just as in the spring of the year). Learning is revived, genius appears, industrial revolutions occur, crops are good, and times are prosperous.

WARM-WET

The warm-wet period sees the climax of the trends started in the previous transition, with achievement becoming organized, and the emphasis put on cooperation and integration of views and effort rather than individual accomplishment. Interest in the state rather than the individual develops and governments become more rigid and centralized.

WARM-DRY

As the weather changes from a general warm-wet phase to warm-dry phase, the rigid governments of the previous period become despotic, police states emerge and personal freedom declines. Behavior patterns are introverted. In art, surrealistic and impressionistic patterns develop, and in business, aggressiveness and self-confidence decline with subsequent depressions and the collapse of economic systems.

During the transition to the next cold period, according to Wheeler, wars reflect the culmination of the decadence of the previous period and become the cruelest type of struggle with entire populations slaughtered or enslaved. (This period saw the beginning of World War II.) However, as the temperature falls and rainfall increases, activity increases, crops are again good, and general revival begins.

COLD-WET

The cold-wet phase sees the reemergence of individualistic philosophy, with decentralizing trends in government and business. It is a period of emancipation and natural behavior; art is straightforward and simple; scholarship follows mechanistic lines. These trends continue and grow until they reach a climax of general anarchy during the cold-dry period to follow.

If we are now into the cold-dry period, we can eagerly look forward to the golden age of the warm-wet period coming up next. And the sooner the better!

OUR SHUDDERING EARTH

Lake Hebgen, twelve miles west of Yellowstone Park, is a favorite watering hole and resting place for waterfowl and other bird life.

At noon on August 16, 1959, every bird began to leave the area and by nightfall not a bird was to be seen on the lake. This event was so unusual that it aroused both local and national scientific interest. At midnight the first shocks of Yellowstone's frightening earthquake began just west of the park.

What mysterious force caused the birds to abandon the area twelve hours before the first earth tremors? Dr. John Aldrich of the Department of the Interior searched all available literature on the subject but failed to find any record of similar behavior in the past. Although birds are known to be acutely sensitive to changes of atmospheric pressure, one wonders from what source came the early warning of impending disaster. How did the birds know that Lake Hebgen soon would not be a safe resting place?

More than a million earthquakes occur annually throughout the world and are registered on sensitive seismographs with ratings in intensity from 1 to 10. Earthquakes originate miles beneath the surface of the earth, splitting tremendous masses of rock along rupture planes called "faults." They recur in the same well-defined areas year after year, especially along the Pacific coast, the western mountain region of the United States, and a large part of Canada.

That they occur in the same area time after time is common knowledge. But there is growing evidence that their behavior has a rhythmic pattern, and increased research and knowledge into possible earthquake cycles may save the world countless lives and billions of dollars in property damage.

Dr. Charles Davison, of England, studied records of earthquakes in the northern hemisphere for the years 1305 to 1899. During this 581-year period there were fifty-three peaks of earthquake abundance at an average of 10.96 years apart.

Davison found a close association between earthquakes and sunspots, as you can see in Figure 44.

Fig. 44: Earthquakes and Sunspots, 1829–96

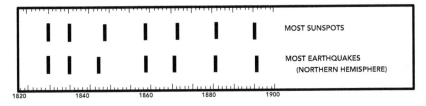

Note that the first cycle is short for both sunspots and earthquakes, the next cycle is average for both, the third is long for both, and so on (after Davison). Is there some association between earthquakes and sunspots, and when we discover it, will we have another important clue as to how cycles operate?

He noted that earthquakes and sunspots both fluctuate in a cycle about eleven years long and that the ideal time of *most* quakes is about the same as the ideal time of *most* sunspots. Also, the irregularities of the eleven-year earthquake cycle seem to be similar to the irregularities of the eleven-year sunspot cycle. Perhaps there is some association between earthquakes and sunspots. What is it?

When we discover it, will it throw light on the way cycles operate and the cause of cycles in other things?

The sun and its fascinating behavior are closely related to our weather in many ways. We will take a long look at these meteorological "coincidences" later.

Many other cycles have been discovered in earthquakes. In Japan, where the earth trembles several times a day, the great seismologist Omori discovered an increase in numbers every 2.75 years. Stanford University's president, following the California earthquake of 1906, concluded that earthquakes in the Portola rift appeared to have a thirty-to-forty-year cycle, and a former Weather Bureau meteorologist, W. C. Clough, working with 1,700 years of data, alleged the existence of a thirty-seven-year cycle in the behavior of Chinese earthquakes. I tested his theory, refined the cycle length to thirty-five years, and discovered an additional significant cycle that measured 17.66 years.

Volcanos spew their "fire and brimstone" on land and man with little warning. Most famous perhaps is Vesuvius, which erupted in A.D. 79 and buried the metropolis of Pompeii under twenty feet of pumice stone and ash. Vesuvius still belches approximately every thirty seconds.

Although volcanos are scattered throughout the world, the majority are in the Pacific Ocean area. Unfortunately, accurate records for their eruption are available only for this century so that any study of their cycles is extremely limited. Yet the volcanologist Giuseppe Imbo stated that eruptions of Vesuvius occur at intervals approximately fourteen to seventeen years apart, although he too claimed that there were not sufficient data to make firm predictions.

However, T. A. Jaggar, who was one of the world's outstanding authorities on volcanic activity and lived on the edge of the crater of the volcano Kilauea in Hawaii, had marked success with his predictions. In January 1929 he successfully predicted the eruption of Kilauea. In 1945 he repeated his forecast, and again Kilauea erupted. The striking features of the Kilauea pattern, according to Jaggar, were a long cycle of 134 years, another of approximately 33 years, and a minor cycle of approximately 11 years. The 11-year cycle, he noted, showed a tendency to correspond to the minimum period of spots on the sun.

California's Lassen Peak is the most recently active peak in the conterminous United States and it shows evidence of a sixty-five-year cycle. A major eruption occurred in the period from 1914 to 1917, and according to the geologist H. A. Harkness, an earlier eruption took place in the winter of 1850–51. Other geologists corroborate his dating and allege that there is good reason to believe that sixty-five years earlier another outbreak occurred.

Based on this brief evidence, if the cycle continues, there should be a very hot year near Lassen Peak around 1980.

THE BILLION-DOLLAR BASIN

The Great Lakes are the largest inland body of fresh water in the world, encompassing in a "basin" approximately 295,000 square miles of land and water. The five lakes forming this great natural wonder exhibit the same behavior that one notices in most other phenomena in nature. Their lake levels go up and down in cycles, creating havoc with shipping, fishing, beach resorts, and the manufacture of electric power.

In 1964, when the water level of the Great Lakes had reached its lowest point in history, a congressional hearing was called and Senator Philip Hart's opening remarks contained an analogy pertinent to our inquiry: "The Basin is the heart of the Midcontinent . . . in fact, the heart of the American continent. It is a heart which beats in direct ratio to the strength and capacity and continued availability of that water."

Colonel S. W. Pinnell, of the Army Corps of Engineers, testified during the hearings. He explained that the water levels in the Great

Lakes depend primarily on such natural processes as precipitation, runoff, and evaporation. If there is a major variation in these normal processes, there is a corresponding change in the net amounts of water supplied to the lakes, and this results in consequent periods of abnormally high or low water.

The major economic effects of low water level on commerce and power were also explained. Colonel Pinnell said that a major portion of commercial shipping on the Great Lakes is affected by the low levels of Lakes Michigan and Huron. From an analysis of major items of lake traffic into or out of United States harbors during 1964, when water levels were about one foot too low, he noted that the loss in commercial shipping was estimated at about $7 million. Also, reductions in power generation occur because when levels are low the outflow from the lakes is low. During the first half of 1964 the output of the state generating plant at Niagara was about 1¼ billion kilowatt-hours less than average.

Colonel Harry A. Musham, of Chicago, has been forecasting *future* levels of Lakes Michigan and Huron for many years with considerable success. In 1941 he predicted that Lake Michigan would reach maximum levels in 1951 and 1952. It did. In 1943 he predicted that lake levels would decline in 1963, *twenty years later*. They did—to a point that brought about the aforementioned congressional investigation.

Musham's forecasts, which he arrived at after studying data on the levels in Lakes Michigan and Huron, are based on a cycle that he says may be about 22.75 years long. Michigan and Huron have the same water level, and changes in their levels are generally indicative of changes in the other Great Lakes. Musham extends his relationship beyond the Great Lakes, saying, "What happens in Lake Michigan is an index of what is happening, fresh water-wise, throughout the world's bread basket regions. Like all other landlocked reservoirs, the lake is fed by rain. Studies show that Great Lakes' peak levels are always preceded by bountiful worldwide precipitation."

A comprehensive scanning of the data for Lake Huron and Lake Michigan recently made at the Foundation tends to confirm Musham's work and suggests a number of cycles in these figures. The post-1964 upturn in lake levels predicted by these cycles has indeed come about.

A complete understanding of the cycles in the levels of the Great Lakes would contribute greatly to the ability of hydrologists to forecast future lake levels. The saving that would result from this knowledge when applied to the stabilization of lake levels, minimizing damage done to shore installations, controlling harbor depths, and many other areas is incalculable.

Since precipitation is so closely related to lake levels, increased knowledge could also aid in making more accurate long-range weather forecasts, with subsequent reductions in agricultural losses. The importance of knowing in advance the basic climate pattern—wet or dry, hot or cold—for a large area of the country does not need stating.

But it does need to be pointed out that the problem of long-range weather forecasting, even with recent advances in equipment and techniques, is far from being solved, and the possibility of cycles being a large part of the solution should not be overlooked.

"The human tragedy reaches its climax in the fact that after all the exertions and sacrifices of hundreds of millions of people ... we lie in the grip of even worse perils than those we have surmounted."

—Winston Churchill

11

The Patterns of War

WHY ARE PEOPLE so intrigued by the subject of cycles? One reason is that a knowledge of cycles throws light on the probabilities of the future.

However, interest in the subject runs deeper than this. There seems to be a craving within the human heart to find regularity, dependability, and pattern in the universe. This craving may be at the bottom of much of scientific research.

Thus the importance of cycles may lie in the fact that they show us that there is law, order, structure, and pattern in things such as stock and commodity prices, industrial production, war, and many other things previously thought structureless.

In general, the study of cycles is the study of pattern, and pattern is one of half a dozen building blocks from which the universe is constructed. Of these building blocks the three most important may be pattern, space, and time.

Without time the universe would have had no duration. It would have come and gone in an instant.

Without space, it would have been merely a dot, a point.

Without pattern, it would have had no form. It would have been a jumble—one big fog.

Also important to the existence of the universe as we know it are matter and energy. Since Einstein and the atom bomb we know that matter and energy are different forms of the same things, or rather, interchangeable forms. But there is some reason to think that even matter and energy are merely patterns of time and space. It doesn't all boil down to space, time, and pattern, but these three are basic, and the most important of the three may well be pattern.

Pattern is of two main kinds: patterns of space and patterns of time. The two are often related as, for example, in the rat-tat-tat of a boy's stick dragged along a picket fence. The noise is a *pattern* in time; the fence is a *pattern* in space.

Pattern can be simple, like the beat of a tom-tom; or complex, like the variation of light and shade and form and motion in a young forest on a sunny summer day.

The same patterns can often be traced in many other things: the snowflake and the honeycomb, to take a simple example, or the golden mean, more technically known as the logarithmic spiral, which can be traced in such diverse things as leaf arrangement, geologic ages, the curve of a ram's horn or a conch shell, a Beethoven concerto, and even historical events like commodity and stock prices.

One particular kind of pattern, common to both patterns of space and patterns of time, is *recurrence*. Civilizations are born, develop, mature, stabilize, and die. Art forms recur time and time again in various cultures. Myths and symbols recur time and again.

War, man's most ignoble pursuit, has unmistakable patterns of recurrence. What is it that causes us, at rhythmic intervals, to behave worse than the lowest form of animal life? What forces make us act as we do? How do we receive their commands? Why do we follow such a deadly pattern? And why does this pattern manifest itself in cycles?

When we learn what these forces are, and how they work, we

will be able to use them to our advantage. If we know about them, we can, hopefully, circumvent them. If not, we can adapt to them.

People often say, "With cycles as inevitable as they are, isn't it hopeless to try to do anything about them?"

The answer is: "Absolutely not! The cyclic *force* may be inevitable, but the cyclic *result* in many instances is subject to our will—if we know in advance about the force."

Let me give you some examples.

There is absolutely nothing we can do about the *force* that creates the cycle of day and night. However, we can *adapt* to it like the tiger by developing keener eyesight in the dark. Or we can *thwart* the darkness of night by fires, rushes, candles, lamps, and electric lights.

There is nothing we can do about the force that creates summer and winter, but we can *adapt* to it by growing fur. Or we can *thwart* this force by shelters (igloos, huts, tents, houses), clothing, and fires in the winter, and by shade, fans, and air conditioning in the summer.

There is nothing we can do about the tidal forces, but we *adapt* to them by building floating docks. We can even *thwart* this force as did the people of Boston and Cambridge when they put a dam across the Charles River tidal basin, thereby transforming the 12½-hour recurrence of a stinking mud flat into a beautiful lake.

Similarly, *if we know about them*, we can transform the effects of other cycles.

YOUR SEVENTH SENSE

How many senses do you have? Sight, hearing, touch, taste, and smell. Five? Is that all?

Dr. Joseph Banks Rhine, formerly of Duke University and now head of the Foundation for Research on the Nature of Man, has spent the greater part of his lifetime seeking a possible sixth sense in human beings, a sense that enables us, with some degree of accuracy, to read other people's minds or to know things it is impossible to know merely through our conventional five senses, such as the order of cards in a shuffled deck.

I have spent the greater part of my lifetime trying to discover a *seventh sense*, which enables us to detect and respond to certain forces, possibly electromagnetic, in our environment.

It is this seventh sense, if it exists, that may lead us to the insane behavior that culminates in wars, stock market crashes, depressions, civil riots, and moral chaos.

Why do we have this seventh sense if it is bad for us? It probably wasn't bad for us in our earlier stages of development, as it probably helped us survive against the elements and prehistoric beasts.

Early man presumably gained by the recurring exhilarations and depressions caused by these energy waves. The time has now come, however, when man must learn about these forces so that he can adapt himself to them before he becomes as extinct as the dinosaur.

Our work makes it abundantly clear that, directly or indirectly, man is attuned to something like electric signals or magnetic waves. It is true that for the most part he does not "hear" these signals, but they *do* affect him and they *do* cause many of the disturbances to which he is now subjected.

And the greatest of these is war.

WAR, OUR WAY OF LIFE

Man is the most aggressive and deadly animal in the world.

Unlike other animals who normally will kill only for food or in self-defense, man will commit murder singly or en masse in a war with little provocation or motive. In the past 3,400 years the world has known little more than 200 years of absolute peace. But even war, habitual as it may be, is not a continuous thing with us.

It occurs in cycles—and I consider the work I have done in respect to cycles in war by all odds the most important achievement of my lifetime. Yet our research and discoveries in this most important of all human behaviors would not have borne fruit without the monumental efforts of the late Professor Raymond H. Wheeler.

As already mentioned, Professor Wheeler, a professor of psychology at the University of Kansas and president of the Kansas Academy of Sciences, summarized all of recorded history. His War Indexes were an incidental byproduct of that work. History books and historians have always made much of war, so Professor Wheeler and his staff were able to assemble in their Indexes of International War Battles and Civil War Battles the longest, most complete, and most precisely dated series of figures that exists in all recorded history.

Wheeler's method of compiling his index was to assign numerical ratings to every recorded battle. To a mild engagement he gave a value of one, to a moderately severe engagement he gave a value of two, and to a very heavy engagement he assigned a value of three. By adding all these battle ratings for a twelve-month period, one would have a numerical rating for that particular year that could be plotted on a graph.

The War Index was used by Professor Wheeler to show a relationship between shifting temperatures in the earth's climate and man's proclivity for war. Warm periods, he noted, were the time of dictators and international wars, while cold periods produced civil unrest and democracy. His compilations were made without any preconceived notions of cycles, but he did note that there were recurrences of drought and civil war at approximately 170-year intervals and that every third of these drought–civil war periods was more pronounced, thus creating a longer cycle of 510 years. He also observed shorter rhythms, especially one of approximately twenty-three years.

DO WARS COME IN CYCLES?

Soon after North Korean infantry and tanks crossed the 38th parallel on June 25, 1950, those of us connected with the Foundation for the Study of Cycles were confronted, countless times each day, with one question: "Do wars come in cycles?" As the Foundation's director, I found it almost impossible to give an interview or address a group without having to reply to this same query. My reply, which was that they had always come this way in the past, was not sufficient. It satisfied neither the interrogator nor myself.

Then we discovered Professor Wheeler and his Index of International War Battles, and late in 1950 we began our research into the cycles of war—research that still continues, and now at a considerably accelerated pace because of computers.

During those early days a frieze hung on one wall of my study. It was nearly sixteen feet in length and showed every single battle of recorded history from 600 B.C. to A.D. 1952. The frieze consisted of enlargements of charts prepared by Professor Wheeler. For each year little battles, wherever they occurred in the world, were shown by short blocks, medium-sized battles were shown by medium-length blocks, and major engagements were shown by long blocks. These blocks, piled on one another, created a single long vertical bar that indicated the severity of man's warlike behavior for that particular year. Think of a big city skyline at twilight and you will have a fairly accurate picture of what my frieze looked like.

By 1952 I had identified and isolated four cycles in the Index of International Battles.

THE 142-YEAR CYCLE IN WAR

As you can see in this amazing chart (Figure 45), since A.D. 1100, international battles have tended to come in rhythmic cycles that average 142 years in length. (For some unknown reason, from 600

B.C. to A.D. 900 the major cycle in war averaged about 163.5 years in length. No other figures that I know of have switched cycles like this. It is very baffling.)

This 142-year pattern calls for a more than average number of battles for the seventy-one-year period from 1914 to 1985 and a less than average number of battles for the seventy-one-year period from 1985 to 2056.

If, as Professor Wheeler and others believe, there is a relationship between climate and man's belligerency, there may be cycles of about 142 years in various physical reflections of our climate here on earth. These may include the alternate thickness and thinness of tree rings, the thicknesses of sedimentary rock deposits, and the flood levels of great rivers like the Nile, where records are available back over hundreds of years.

Fig. 45: The 142-Year Cycle in International Battles, 1050–1915

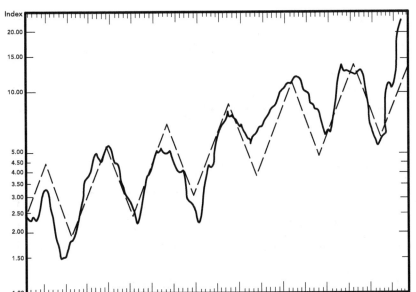

THE 57-YEAR CYCLE IN WAR

In January 1951 I reported on a 57-year cycle (Figure 46) in war. Although the figures in my possession at the time enabled me to trace this cycle backward through only three complete cycles, I pointed out that the wave was clear enough so that prudent men could not ignore the possibility that the next twenty-five or thirty years would see an increasing number of international battles.

THE 22⅕-YEAR CYCLE IN WAR

In February 1951 I reported on a twenty-two-year cycle in war. At first, I had traced it back through twenty-five repetitions to the year 1400 (Figure 47).

Fig. 46: The 57-Year Cycle in International Battles, 1765–1930

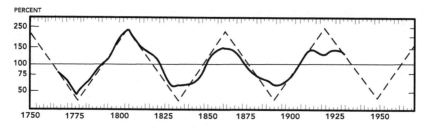

Fig. 47: The 22⅕-Year Cycle in International Battles, 1415–1930

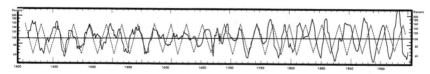

Then, in 1956, I traced it all the way back to 600 B.C., and I had the longest continuous series of waves I had ever found—*116 repetitions of a cycle over a period of 2,500 years!* The odds of this cycle occurring purely by chance are only 8 in 10,000. The continuous presence of a cycle of this length for 2,500 years explodes the idea that wars come when a new generation that does not know the horror of war grows up. Behavior resulting from such a cause could not *possibly* be as regular as this. Remember that these are worldwide figures. Only in the last few years have we had worldwide wars. Over the years war weariness in Greece, let us say, could not possibly account for war weariness in China. Moreover, even for one country war weariness could not possibly, by itself, maintain a constant cycle continuously in step with previous war weariness in other centuries. Some accidental factors would make a war come early or late, and a new timing for war weariness would result.

In the years since its discovery the length of this particular cycle has been refined to 21.98 years.

THE 11⅕-YEAR CYCLE IN WAR

The 11⅕-year cycle (Figure 48) has also been traced back to 600 B.C. It could not have been chance more often than 18 times in 10,000. It has recently been refined to an average wavelength of 11.241 years.

THE WAR PREDICTION

In June 1952 I combined the 142-year cycle, the 57-year cycle, the 22⅕-year cycle, and the 11⅕-year cycle (see Figure 49).

The combination (synthesis), as represented by the bottom heavy line of Figure 49, was then projected into the future as a forecast.

Fig. 48: The 11⅕-Year Cycle in International Battles, 1760–1947

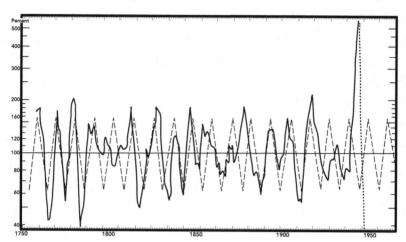

This forecast has come true for the main structure of international battles, for seventeen years! Here is another chart (Figure 50) showing the synthesis (broken line) projected to 1975 compared with the actual index to 1958, its most recent value.

Of course, this forecast was very crude. It used very few cycles. It used no cycles shorter than eleven years, which is like trying to paint a portrait with the foot of an elephant for a brush. All the forecast really said is that times would be rough the world over, in the 1960's, with the possibility that there would be a double peak, the first one in the early sixties and the second one at the end of the decade. The middle 1970's should be reasonably peaceful.

As things actually unfolded, there was a bit of a peak in the first half of the 1960's (India and China, Holland and Indonesia, Syria and Egypt, Tibet and China, etc.), but, of course, these minor skirmishes were completely overshadowed in the latter part of the 1960's by the war in Vietnam.

Since the work of 1952 four additional cycles in war have been discovered. Three, with average wavelengths of 17.71, 17.31, and 5.98 years, have been traced all the way back to 600 B.C. The fourth cycle has a most unusual pattern. It alternates between 9.6-year cycles (remember the Canadian lynx?) and 12.35-year cycles for spans of 86.4 years, each clearly visible in the War Index, wave by wave, since A.D. 562. These cycles, and others that we now have hints of, will undoubtedly modify the original projection made in 1952.

Fig. 49: The War Cycles, combined, 1930–70

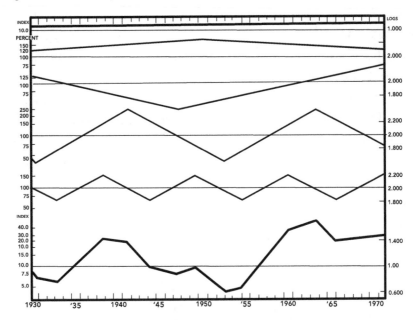

This chart depicts (reading from the top down) the trend of wars, the 142-year, the 57-year, the 22½-year, and the 11⅓-year cycles. The bottom heavy line brings all these elements together in a synthesis or combination.

THE BEHAVIOR OF WARS

There is one aspect in the cycles of war that I find particularly fascinating. International battles clearly have their counterparts in *both* biological and economic cycles. By a "biological" cycle I mean one that expresses itself predominantly in biological phenomena, such as animal abundance. By an "economic" cycle I mean one that expresses itself predominantly in economic phenomena, such as prices and production. It is rare indeed for a phenomenon to evidence both kinds of cycles, *but war does*. For example, the 9.6-year cycle in war can also be found in forty-two different biological phenomena. On the other hand, the 17.7-year cycle in war is primarily an economic cycle.

As international war is sensitive to cyclic forces that are normally responded to only by animals and also to cyclic forces that are normally responded to only by men in their economic capacity, we may think of it as both an economic *and* a biological phenomenon. This is most interesting and unusual.

If we knew the particular aspect of animals, or of men, that responds to cyclic forces and the aspect of man as a producer and investor that responds to different cyclic forces, we might have an additional clue as to the causes and nature of war cycles in general.

Fig. 50: Index of International Battles, 1820–1958

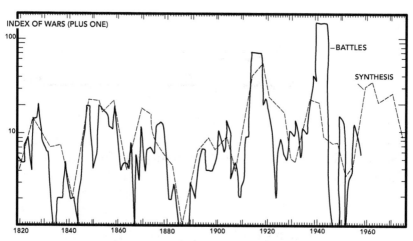

The solid line represents the actual Index of International Battles, plus one. The broken line is the synthesis, or combination of cycles from the bottom of Figure 49 extended backward for 90 years to 1820. As you will note, even with the use of only four cycles, the synthesis comes fairly close to depicting the ebb and flow of international battles over this span of time.

How should we interpret these war cycles? In my own mind I picture the space in which we live as filled with forces that alternately stimulate and depress all human beings—make them more or less optimistic, or make them more or less fearful. These forces do not *control* us, they merely *influence* us. They create a *climate* that is sometimes more favorable to war and sometimes less favorable. War will come without the stimulus of these forces and wars will be avoided in spite of these stimuli, but, *on the average*, the probabilities for war are greater when the "climate" is right.

The evidence suggests that one of the major causes of war, if not the major cause, may be mass hysteria or combativeness, which occurs at reasonably regular rhythmic intervals.

What mysterious forces cause these war cycles, how they operate, and how we can control them—or their effects—may, in this nuclear age, be the most important discovery ever made by man.

"Only by understanding the mechanism which connects him to the earth and the sky will man be able to understand his physical and psychic position in the universe today. In the context of the universe as it is, man will find his natural role."

—Giorgio Piccardi

12

Cycles in the Universe

IF CYCLES ARE not merely accidental, and if they are caused by forces outside the earth, there are three possible sources: the sun, the planets, and energy from outer space. No one of these, as I see it, is any more fantastic or improbable than the others. All should be investigated with equal impartiality.

Once, when mentioning the planets as a possible cause for some of the cycles observed on earth, I was taken to task by a good friend. "That's astrology," he said. "If you talk like that people will think you are an astrologer. You will lose your scientific standing. You will bring discredit upon the Foundation. Don't you know that astrology is completely discredited and that therefore the planets could have nothing whatever to do with it?"

Of course I know that astrology is completely discredited. The idea that planets could have any effect upon the events of *individual* lives, according to their time of birth, is so fantastic that science has rejected it out of hand without even bothering to investigate it. The mere suggestion that it be investigated would damn any scientist, and if his findings were favorable, I am sure no scientific journal would publish his work.

Astrology is something like a religion. It is a belief, or a set of beliefs, handed down from antiquity. It was an accepted belief as late as the 1600's. Even Kepler took it for granted. Science has now relegated it to the realm of folklore, chiefly because astrologers have not used the methods of science to try to prove their case nor have they been able to explain satisfactorily how any such planetary influence on individual lives could possibly exist or operate.

In many ways astrology is similar to alchemy, the medieval forerunner of chemistry. Alchemy, too, was a set of beliefs, specifically that elements could be transmuted, or changed, one into the other if only one knew enough. Making gold from lead was the main objective.

Of course, essentially *this has now been done*. Elements *have* been transmuted, but at a prohibitive cost. But suppose, when the scientists started to work on the project of converting one element into another, someone had said, "Stop! The old alchemists believed that. Don't you know that the belief that elements can be transmuted is alchemy?"

If someone had said that to our modern nuclear physicists, they would have replied, "Of course we know! When it's a *belief*, it is nothing but a superstition, but when it's a proved and demonstrated fact, it's science. It isn't the *subject matter* that governs, but the *method* of study and evaluation. The fact that someone has a belief in something should not make the subject matter taboo!"

My investigation of a possible connection between planetary cycles and earthly cycles, if I should ever have time to make it, would have nothing to do with astrological beliefs. It would have nothing to do with birthdates and other mumbo jumbo. It would concern electromagnetic or similar forces in the universe that might affect weather and various life processes, including human beings *in the mass*. Let us conjecture for a moment before we look up into the universe in search of more cycles.

THE LONG WAVES

Gamma rays, ultraviolet light, X-rays, infrared rays, visible light, radio waves, and secondary cosmic rays are all grouped together as "electromagnetic radiation." Gamma rays and X-rays can go right through you and, in large doses, can destroy your tissues. Visible light is what we all see with our eyes. Infrared rays can burn us, while radio waves cause us no obvious harm. However, all these waves of the spectrum have one thing in common; they travel from their source to the receiver at the speed of light, 186,000 miles per second! A spectrum giving the wavelength and frequency of all these different waves, as compiled by Compton and Caldwell and published in *Radio Today*, is shown in Figure 51.

Fig. 51: Electromagnetic Wave Spectrum

If you will look closely you will note the word "visible" printed vertically between the infrared and ultraviolet bands. *Every other frequency is invisible to the naked eye except this tiny portion of the spectrum.*

While every type of electromagnetic radiation travels at the same speed, the number of cycles per second at which these various waves oscillate (in cycles) varies from a cycle of one or two per second at the left of our spectrum to 100 billion billion per second and beyond as we move toward the gamma and secondary cosmic rays.

Now—and this is pure conjecture—if we have electromagnetic

waves that come a trillionth of a second apart, a billionth of a second apart, a millionth of a second apart, and a thousandth of a second apart, why can't there be electromagnetic waves that come even less frequently, let's say a thousand seconds apart, a million seconds apart, a billion seconds apart? A thousand seconds would be about sixteen minutes, a million seconds would be about 11½ days, a billion seconds would be about 31½ days.

If there are electromagnetic waves oscillating throughout our universe with these longer lengths, how else would we know of their existence *except by our observing their influence on earth*? Certainly no electrical devices in the laboratories are going to tune in to waves that are several years from crest to crest. But such waves may be affecting plants, animals, and human beings, either directly or indirectly. The indirect effect might be brought about through weather or through an effect upon the sun. This, in turn, might influence plants, animals, and human beings by means of variations of ultraviolet light or other radiations.

And where do these long waves originate? Let me repeat: They can come only from the sun, the planets, or outer space. They can come only from "somewhere out there."

PRISONER FOR LIFE

Our earth is held prisoner by a small yellow star that is hurtling through space at fantastic speeds toward a dark void between the constellations of Hercules and Lyra.

Held in rein by a gravitational pull strong enough to snap a steel cable thicker than the United States is wide, we are in complete bondage to the sun, in spite of the 93 million miles that separate us. Were the sun to vanish tomorrow, all life on our planet would cease within a very short span of time.

As you read these words you are traveling so fast to maintain your relationship with that flaming ball of fiery gas that it may be impossible for you to comprehend it.

First of all, your earth is rotating, relative to the stars, in a cycle of 23 hours, 56 minutes, 4.09 seconds. In order to accomplish one complete rotation, each day, our earth is spinning at a speed that has been measured at 1,000 miles per hour at the equator.

Our earth is also revolving around the sun in a cycle of 365.242 days. In order to accomplish this complete orbit around the sun, each year, our earth is traveling at a speed of 66,000 miles per hour!

Our sun, with us and eight other planets and many moons in tow, circles our galaxy, the Milky Way, in a cycle of 230 million years. In order to accomplish this cycle it moves at a speed of 481,000 miles per hour.

Lastly, our Milky Way galaxy is moving around a supercluster of thousands of galaxies at a speed of 1,350,000 miles per hour. So, without even mussing your hair, you are at this moment spinning around at speeds up to 1,000 miles per hour on a ball that is flying at 66,000 miles per hour around a sun that is traveling 481,000 miles per hour around a Milky Way that is rocketing at 1,350,000 miles per hour around a supercluster of galaxies. And all of this in a pattern of cycles so exact that it is possible to predict our position in the universe a thousand years from today.

THE MYSTERIOUS SUNSPOT CYCLES

Science has acquired much knowledge about our sun since Epicurus, in 300 B.C., made his profound, but inaccurate, announcement that the sun was apparently a fiery ball with a diameter of only two feet. Now we know that it is slightly more than 865,000 miles in diameter, 109 times the diameter of our earth, and its mass has been estimated at *2 billion billion billion tons*. Approximately 99 percent of all the matter in our solar system is part of the sun, and this matter is burning at the rate of 4 million tons per second, spewing vast amounts of energy far into space.

The sun's density is only 1½ times that of water, and its temperature on the surface is approximately 6,000 degrees centigrade. At its center the density is many times that of steel and the temperature is many millions of degrees centigrade. Its gravitational pull is so immense that if you could stand on the sun's surface without becoming an instant cinder you would weigh in the neighborhood of two tons.

Both the sun and the moon rotate in cycles of about twenty-seven days, except that the sun does not behave like a solid body in its rotation. At its equator the period of rotation is twenty-five days, while it is thirty-one days at a solar latitude of 75 degrees. Why its larger middle should rotate *more slowly* than the smaller latitudes near its poles is a mystery that science is still struggling to explain.

But our sun's greatest mystery is its sunspots and their cycles.

Astrophysicists are not yet in full agreement as to what sunspots are, and they have no explanation as to their cause or why they should appear in greater numbers in a cycle that has averaged a little over eleven years for as far back as records are available (300 B.C.).

However, let us accept the definition that sunspots are whirling vortices of cooler, seemingly dark gas that blemish the surface of the sun. They can appear singly or in groups, but they usually show up in pairs. Their size can be immense. One group, which appeared in 1946, covered an area sufficient to swallow over 100 earths.

Sunspots are sometimes accompanied by bright flares spitting thousands of miles into the corona and emitting strong doses of ultraviolet, charged particles, and X-rays. Science has no theory, as yet, to explain the flares satisfactorily.

Sunspots usually appear and vanish within a few days but frequently they endure for many months, disappearing from our view with each rotation of the sun and reappearing again approximately two weeks later.

Sunspots are also magnetic, and one of their most mysterious characteristics is that when they are in pairs or small groups they act as if they were the positive and negative poles of huge horseshoe magnets embedded in the sun. In one cycle the leading spots of each pair or group in the northern hemisphere will have a positive polarity while the leading spots in the southern hemisphere will have a negative polarity. In the next cycle the situation reverses itself and the leading spots in the northern hemisphere will be negative while the leading spots in the southern hemisphere will be positive.

The ancient Chinese knew about sunspots and Galileo mentioned them over 300 years ago. In 1825 a German amateur astronomer, Heinrich Schwabe, using a small two-inch telescope, began observing the sun in his search for a planet within the orbit of Mercury. Soon he became so fascinated by the ever-changing blemishes on the sun that he abandoned his original goal and commenced to keep records of the number of sunspots that appeared. In 1843 he announced that the number of sunspots fluctuated in a pattern approximately ten years long.

Schwabe's announcement caused hardly a ripple in astronomical circles until Humboldt described the cycle in his monumental work, *The Cosmos*. Eventually even the Royal Astronomical Society recognized Schwabe's long years of quiet research and awarded him their gold medal. Since 1940 the Foundation for the Study of Cycles has devoted considerable study to the subject of sunspot cycles and we have been able to refine Schwabe's early findings to the point where we have fixed the average sunspot cycle length since 1527 at 11.11 years (see Figure 52).

Fig. 52: Average Annual Sunspot Numbers, 1700–1968

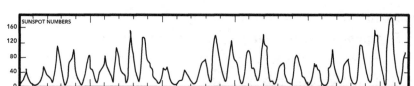

In the past century attempts have been made to link nearly every behavior on this planet to these mysterious eruptions.

Do sunspots cause cycles here on earth? My answer, whenever I am asked (which is often), is that sunspots appear to cause some of them. For example, consider Figure 53, which shows, by means of the lower curve, the number of sunspots each year from 1835 to 1930. The upper curve indicates the variations of magnetism here on earth during the same period. The correspondence is striking and is generally accepted as proof that sunspots affect magnetic conditions here on earth.

Fig. 53: Sunspots and Terrestrial Magnetism, 1835–1930

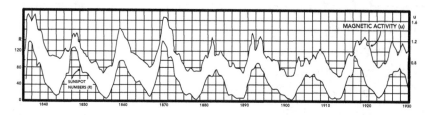

The upper curve shows magnetic activity. The lower curve shows sunspot numbers over the same period of time. Note the close correspondence between the two.

SUNSPOTS AND US

In 1878 a British economist, W. Stanley Jevons, advanced a hypothesis that sunspots caused "commercial crises." He believed that the variations in the number of sunspots produced corresponding variations in crops and that *through this channel* cycles in business were triggered. Jevons' work was based, in part, on the earlier writings of Dr. Hyde Clarke, who had described an eleven-year cycle in speculation and famine.

In 1934 two Harvard research workers, Carlos Garcia-Mata and Felix Shaffner, set out to prove that Jevons was wrong. Armed with a research grant, they intended to establish that there was no relationship between business, stock prices, agricultural crops, and sunspots. There was indeed no relationship between sunspots and crops, but to their great surprise they found a very close correspondence between sunspots and manufacturing and production. This relationship covered the period 1875–1931 and was very marked. However, the highs and lows of the sunspot cycles came *after* the highs and lows of manufacturing and total production. You can see this in Figure 54.

Fig. 54: Sunspots and Manufacturing, 1875–1931

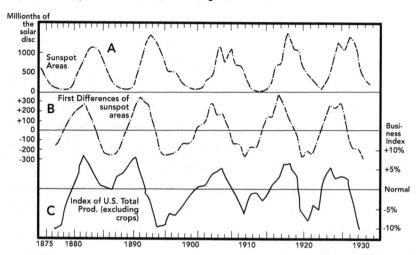

Sunspot areas and first differences (a measure of rate of change) of sunspot areas compared to manufacturing production, U.S.A., all values smoothed by 4-year moving averages. Note the dramatic correspondence between B and C.

Of course, the supposed cause can hardly follow the result, so Garcia-Mata and Shaffner reasoned that the *rate of change* in the number of sunspots might be the cause. When the rate of change (B in Figure 54) is compared to the index of total production (C in Figure 54), the correspondence is dramatic.

In 1881 the English astronomer N. R. Pogson traced an intimate connection between sunspot frequency and grain prices in India.

In 1919 Professor Ellsworth Huntington advanced the idea that variations in solar radiation had an effect on human beings and thus, in turn, upon business conditions. His hypothesis ran contrary to the popular belief that business was affected first, with the business conditions then affecting human beings.

In 1936 Loring B. Andrews, a Harvard astronomer, called attention to the apparent correlation over the preceding two hundred years between sunspot activity and wars, international crises, and economic distress. He conjectured that the cause of these and other solar–terrestrial correlations might be either the intensity of solar radiation or emanations of ultraviolet light. Since both of these two solar phenomena are associated with sunspot activity, Andrews felt that a variation in ultraviolet light was the more reasonable of the two possible explanations for the economic and sociological correlations.

In 1965 Charles J. Collins, an investment counselor, published "An Inquiry into the Effect of Sunspot Activity on the Stock Market." In his article he noted that since 1871 the largest stock market declines, percentagewise, coincided with or followed years in which average sunspot numbers reached or exceeded a count of fifty.

THE TIME LAG

The jury is still out on the question of this important link between the earth and sun. No verdict has been reached because of one perplexing fact. Let me give you an example.

In an earlier chapter we discussed the brilliant Russian scientist Tchijevsky and his discovery that, in the mass, our world seems to increase in excitability in a consistent pattern of nine waves per century. His work had involved detailed statistical research into the histories of seventy-two countries.

Tchijevsky found not only that his index was characterized by 11.11-year cycles but that the highs of these cycles tended to correspond with highs in sunspot activity.

In 1960 I made a thorough investigation of Tchijevsky's work, using sunspot data that were not available to Tchijevsky forty years earlier. I discovered that when the years of maximum sunspot activity were compared with the values of Tchijevsky's Index of Mass Human Excitability, the highs of the sunspot cycles *followed* the highs of his Index by an average of about one year.

This time lag often occurs when earthly cycles are compared with sunspots. In general, regardless of period, the sunspot cycles turn *after* the corresponding earthly cycles they are supposed to create. And you cannot have the cause follow the effect!

Can it be that something is causing both the cycles on the sun and the cycles here on earth—but that the sun takes longer to respond?

Could our friends Garcia-Mata and Shaffner be right in that it is the rate of change of sunspot numbers rather than the actual number of spots that is the trigger to our earthly behaviors?

Could it be that since cycles of the same length here on earth tend to have their highs later and later as they occur closer to the equator, and since sunspots normally occur in the lower latitudes, we must take these facts into consideration when trying to relate the two? Most events recorded here on earth with eleven-year cycles occur between 40 degrees and 55 degrees north latitude, while sunspots lie, on the average, at about 14 degrees north and south latitude on the sun, so there would normally be a time lag if the two phenomena were the result of a common cause, and if cycles on the sun behave like cycles on earth.

The evidence in favor of a relationship between solar activity and behavior here on earth is provocative but not yet conclusive. Yet new discoveries seem to be leading us closer and closer to a solution to the great sunspot mystery. One of these new clues, uncovered by C. N. Anderson, of the Bell Telephone Laboratories, followed this logical line of reasoning:

Sunspots increase and decrease in waves that range from seven to seventeen years in length, but which have an average wavelength of 11.11 years. Sunspots normally occur in pairs. Sunspots are magnetized. In one wave of the sunspot cycle positive spots will lead in the sun's northern hemisphere, negative spots will lead in the sun's southern hemisphere.

In the next wave this situation is reversed: Negative spots will lead in the northern hemisphere; positive spots will lead in the southern hemisphere. Thus it takes two sunspot waves—or "cycles," as they are called—for the behavior to come around again to the place of beginning. The period of the double sunspot cycle is thus 22.22 years (see Figure 55).

Fig. 55: The Double Sunspot Cycle, 1700–1968

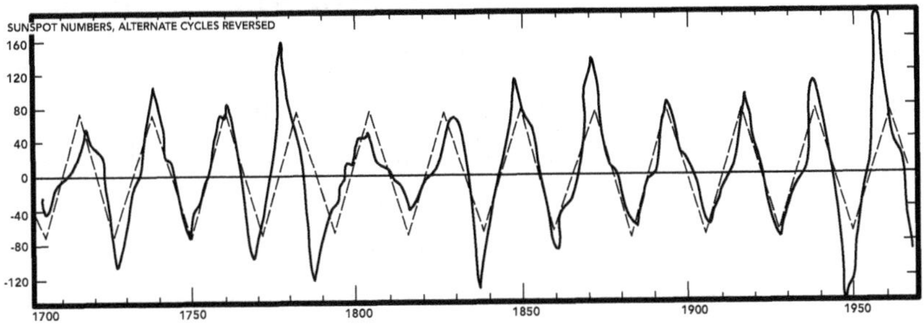

Sunspot numbers with alternate 11.11-year cycles reversed.

The wavelengths of certain average cycles in sunspot numbers with alternate cycles reversed correspond closely with the average times when several of our planets line up with each other as seen from the sun in what is called a "heliocentric planetary conjunction." If further investigation proves this association to be a real one, we will have added importantly to our knowledge of solar system mechanics and to our ability to forecast ordinary sunspot numbers, an ability of increasing importance as we enter the age of space travel with its impending dangers from solar eruptions of all sorts.

THE SOLAR CONSTANT

Dr. C. G. Abbot, of the Smithsonian Institution, has spent the greater part of his lifetime trying to convince meteorologists and scientists in general that the "solar constant" is not constant but fluctuates in cycles instead.

The "solar constant" is a measurement, in calories per square centimeter per minute, of the amount of the sun's energy received. As the name implies, it has little variation, but Dr. Abbot, involved for many years with the measurement of this "constant," noticed what he termed "dent-like depressions," that is, small ups and downs in the measurements.

These tiny ups and downs seemed to fluctuate in a cycle of 273 months—or almost twenty-three years. However, the small variation in the solar constant—only 1 or 2 percent—was a serious stumbling block for the meteorologists, who did not believe that the variations were large enough to account for such changes in the weather as were claimed by Dr. Abbot.

Dr. Abbot proceeded to project his cycles in the solar constant backward and discovered that these cycles corresponded with past weather conditions (Figure 56). Then he began to prepare charts of calculated precipitation or temperature based on his 273-month cycle (Figure 57) and followed this with long-range calculations for fifty-four weather stations. He published numerous papers covering over fifty years of study, and the amount of evidence he marshaled to support his case is impressive.

Fig. 56: Abbot's Cycle of St. Louis Precipitation, 1860–87

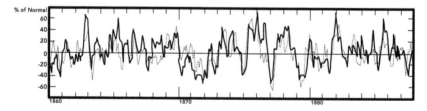

The solid line indicates departures from normal in St. Louis precipitation. The broken line indicates Abbot's combination of various cycles over the same period.

Fig. 57: Various Other Weather Cycles, 1934–39

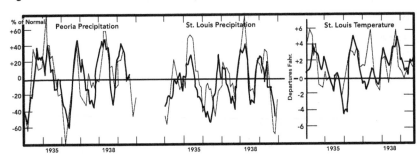

The solid line indicates departures from normal at Peoria and St. Louis and temperature at St. Louis. The broken line indicates Abbot's combination of various cycles over the same period.

H. H. Clayton, chief forecaster of the meteorological service of Argentina, discovered similar correspondences between variations in solar radiation and barometric pressure (Figure 58) after learning of Abbot's work on solar variation. He applied his findings in extensive long-range weather forecasting.

Fig. 58: Solar Radiation at Calama, Chile, April 1920

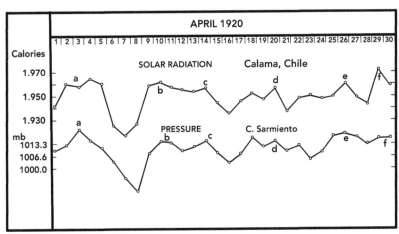

Note the close correspondence between solar radiation and barometric pressure over the same period of time (after Clayton).

Except in Argentina no weather forecasting service attached to any government has ever taken solar variation into account, but I suspect that Dr. Abbot's work will one day have its moment in court.

THE MOON CYCLES

Even before Neil Armstrong and Edwin Aldrin stepped courageously onto the surface of the moon, we "earthlings" had begun to refer to it as the "seventh continent." However, none of the six continents floating placidly on the face of our earth can begin to approach the effects that the moon and its cycles have on our life.

Although the sun is 26 million times larger in mass than the moon, it is 389 times farther away and so the moon exerts a force on us which is 2½ times greater than that of the sun. This tremendous force is most evident in the behavior of our tides. As the moon circles our planet in a cycle of 24 hours and 50½ minutes, high tides and low tides follow each other in most parts of the world every 12 hours and 25 minutes. This gravitational pull is strong enough to lift millions of gallons of water as high as fifty feet in places such as New Brunswick's Bay of Fundy. Since so much of you is water, is it unreasonable to conjecture that the moon's cycles might somehow also "lift" you?

There are three main moon cycles besides the daily one just mentioned. The first is the monthly lunar cycle caused by the revolution of the moon around the earth. The length of this monthly cycle, relative to the sun (from full moon to full moon), is 29.53039 days.

The moon travels around the earth in an ellipse—a flattened circle—with the earth near the center of this ellipse. This ellipse wobbles like a poorly thrown football in a cycle that takes thirty-one years and two or three days (depending on leap years) to return to the point where it started. The axis of this orbit not only wobbles but turns in a counterclockwise direction, making one complete cycle relative to the stars every 3,232.6 days, or 8.85 years.

As you know from watching and reading about our astronauts, the orbit of the moon is not exactly in the same plane as the orbit of the earth. Looking at the two from the side, for half the lunar month the moon is a little above the line connecting earth and sun, and for the other half a little below it. The line where the planes of the two orbits connect is called the line of nodes; this intersection line, relative to the stars, is the same every 18.6 years.

Although man has made great advances in applying his knowledge of the moon to the predicting of tides and their levels, he is only beginning to explore other possible moon–earth relationships, for now it is known that there are tides in the atmosphere that are influenced by the force of the moon. Changes in geomagnetism and radio-field strength appear to follow the changing phase of the moon, and movements of the earth's crust seem to relate to the position of the moon. It has been estimated that the city of Moscow rises and falls nearly twenty inches, twice a day, in response to the moon's gravitational beckoning.

The effect of the moon on our physical environment is now under intensive study, although complete and definite answers are still to come. We have even begun to explore the realm of lunar folklore. The Department of Agriculture has investigated the question of whether planting crops during certain phases of the moon will affect the ensuing growth and yield of the crop. They found that the phase of the moon in which a crop is planted has no relation to its outcome, although folklore may still have its basis in fact. It is said that timber in the tropics must be felled at the correct phase of the moon. If the trees are cut when the moon is waxing, the sap runs heavy and draws beetles that eat the wood. Contracts to cut timber in South America and the South Sea Islands sometimes specify that the wood is to be cut only during the waning phase of the moon.

This phenomenon is not surprising if you will recall the work of H. S. Burr with the electric voltage of trees. Burr drilled tiny holes several feet apart (vertically) on a tree trunk and connected the holes with wire. An electric current flows along such a wire, and Burr has recorded this flow, minute by minute, for many years. The current sometimes flows up and sometimes down. Neither the current nor the voltage is steady, but the same strength of current flows in the same direction at the same time in trees that are miles apart!

The variation in voltage goes in cycles, and one of the cycles observed appears to correlate with the phases of the moon. Of course, the effect of the moon may be direct, or it may be secondary.

Remember Professor Frank Brown and his pieces of potato hermetically sealed in rigid containers under constant conditions of pressure and temperature? They gave evidence, among other things, of a lunar monthly rhythm of oxygen consumption. The rate was lowest at the time of the new moon and went up to a high during the third quarter of the moon.

Thus there is solid evidence that does indicate that plants respond to some extent to the changing phases of the moon. Lunar cycles in plants exist, although research on this phase of the earth–moon system is also in its infancy. It is logical that work on the effect of the moon would start first with the tides, on which our facts are remarkably complete, then move to other physical aspects (air, geomagnetism, etc.), then move to plants and animals, and lastly, concentrate on man—for man hesitates to admit that he is influenced by any environmental forces!

The lunar cycles of life in the sea and on the seashore are obvious. One of the classic examples is the palolo worm of the South Seas. This small native delicacy has an elongated posterior filled with reproductive cells. These posteriors break away from the worm's body, which is lodged in burrows in the coral rock, and swarm to the surface of the sea—but only in early morning for two days during the last quarter of the moon during October and November. How does the palolo know when the moon is in its final quarter—and in just two out of thirteen lunar months?

During April and May, grunions, small edible fish native to the coast of California, throw themselves on the beaches until they nearly cover the white sand. But they do this only after the moon and the sun have cooperated to produce the fortnight's highest high tide. On the beach the female grunions scoop shallow depressions in the wet sand and deposit their eggs. The eggs remain, since later and lesser tides do not disturb them. When the next highest high tide arrives, some fifteen days later, the eggs will hatch and the fry will enter the sea.

What force guides the grunion to deposit its eggs in the sand after the highest tide and not before? And how does it know exactly which tide will be the highest? For if another and stronger tide immediately followed the deposit of eggs, they would be washed from the sand and have no chance to develop.

The effect of moon on man is buried deep in the consciousness of the race. The word *lunacy*, for example, came into use because of a general belief that the moon triggered certain forms of insanity that occurred in phase with the moon.

Sleepwalking is sometimes attributed to the influence of the full moon, and certainly the supposed romantic influence of the moon has been the source of much income to songwriters. In addition to these and other traditional beliefs there is much scientific evidence of the moon's influence on human activity. In 1950 I published a summary of the number of births occurring in the waxing and waning period of the moon. The record covered the period from 1939 to 1944 and was supplied by Curtis Jackson, then Controller of the Methodist Hospital of Southern California. Of the babies born at the hospital during the time covered, 17 percent more were born during the waxing period of the moon than were born during the waning period. In some of the years births in the waxing period of the moon exceed by as much as 25 percent those in the waning period.

What could be the reason for this behavior? Does it imply a cause-and-effect relationship between the moon and amorousness or fertility? Or is there a rhythm in amorousness or fertility that just happens to correspond to the waxing and waning of the moon? The answers to these questions lie in the field of medicine and outside the study of cycles. We can do no more than pose the question. Physical and experimental science must provide the answers.

Dr. William F. Petersen was one of the truly great men I have known in my lifetime. Although primarily a medical doctor, he felt that in addition to acquiring greater knowledge about bacteriology and immunology, it was imperative that we do everything possible to relate man to his environment. He believed that however minor they might be, cosmic influences should be taken into account.

While studying the moon's effect on man, Petersen compared various kinds of vital statistics with various phases of the moon to see if there were any relationships. These statistics included conceptions compared to deaths, the incidence of scarlet fever, the incidence of epileptic attacks, deaths from tuberculosis, and others.

There appeared to be a definite lunar phase to the chart of deaths from tuberculosis, with an increase in deaths after the full moon. Nevertheless, this is only one factor. Certainly, in any individual case, local weather conditions, the condition of the patient, and other related factors are much more important than the phase of the moon. Nevertheless, when put on a lunar axis and smoothed by a three-day moving average, the record of deaths from tuberculosis does show a high seven days after the full moon and a low eleven days before the full moon.

Researchers are constantly accumulating evidence that tends to show that the moon exerts an influence on earthly affairs, both in the physical environment and in plants and animals. As with nearly every other subject in this book, the material I have presented is the smallest of summaries of a subject that requires a complete book of its own.

THE VARIABLE STARS

Our universe is replete with cycle activity. The planets are spinning in cycles; Jupiter completes one rotation every nine hours and fifty minutes while Pluto takes six days, nine hours, and twenty-one minutes to do the same thing. All planets are also revolving around the sun in cycles; Mercury requires only 2.89 months for a round trip while it takes Pluto 2,981 months to complete its tremendous ellipse around our sun. A third type of planetary cycle involves the length of time it takes for any two planets to line up in a straight line with the sun. Our earth is on a straight line with Mercury and the sun every 116 days, while we only manage to get in line with Mars and the sun every 780 days. These conjunctions, of course, offer a great area for finding possible effects on earthly things, but science has pretty much ignored this area of investigation and left it to the astrologers. However, there are enough hints of a possible relationship between periods of conjunction between our earth, the sun, and other planets so that I'm not sure this idea should be left to them.

Several thousand stars also have cycles. They are called variable stars, and their brightness fluctuates in periods that vary from a few hours to several years. Furthermore, the intensity of the light curves of some of these stars fluctuates in the typical zigzag pattern that characterizes many cycles in both solar and earthly phenomena.

For example, refer to Figure 59, reprinted from *Astronomy* by W. T. Skilling and R. S. Richardson, published and copyrighted by Henry Holt and Company. These curves show that the stars to which they refer get brighter and fainter in the sort of pattern that would result if some master hand pulled a reversing switch at more or less regular intervals.

Fig. 59: A Cycle in a Variable Star, 1922–30

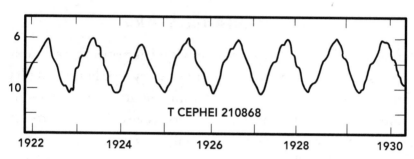

The light curve of the star T Cephei. The wavelength is 387 days.

Variable stars fluctuate in all sorts of wavelengths. The most usual lengths are ½ day, seven days, and 250 days.

What causes the change in brightness of the variable stars? No one really knows.

THE COMET CYCLES

In 1704 the English astronomer Edmund Halley published a paper in which he predicted that a comet that had appeared in 1682 would *reappear* in 1759. It did, and its reappearance established the fact that comets, although they travel in extremely eccentric orbits, have cycles of revolution around the sun. Halley's Comet is scheduled to make its next appearance in 1985.

Hundreds of other lesser-known comets orbit the sun in cyclic trips that are as short as 2.3 years. No one knows how comets originated but astronomers can give you the orbiting cycle for every one so far discovered.

QUASARS, PULSARS, AND CYCLES

Since 1962 two new phenomena have generated tremendous excitement among the world's astronomers.

Quasars (for quasi-stellar radio sources) appear to be closely packed groups of millions of stars, smaller than galaxies. They were first detected by radio telescopes. Apparently they are so distant that, traveling at the speed of light (186,000 miles per second), it has taken 6,000 million light-years for the energy and light from some of them to reach this planet. Radio waves charted at the Jodrell Bank radio telescope in England on June 7, 1966 (Figure 60), began their journey through space over 1,000 million years before the earth came into existence.

Fig. 60: A Cycle in a Quasar

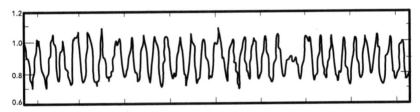

Radio signals received from Quasar CTA 102 as recorded on June 7, 1966. Quasar CTA 102 is believed to be at least 6,000,000,000 light-years away. If this is so, the radio waves causing the deflection of the pen on this record started on their journey through space over 1,000,000,000 years before the earth came into existence (after Sir Bernard Lovell).

I need not point out to you the fairly regular wave or cycle. Quasars are also known to fluctuate in brightness, presenting us with another puzzle. This mysterious aspect is illustrated by Quasar 3c273. It is approximately seven light-years in diameter, which means that it would take seven years for electromagnetic waves to cross the entire quasar. If so, how could the different stars in the quasar all fluctuate in brightness *together*? How could the different stars *know* when to be bright and when to be dim so that separated by billions and billions of miles they still act like a string of bulbs on our Christmas tree, synchronized to blink in unison?

Pulsars are believed to be small balls of debris, only a few miles in diameter, left in space after the explosion of some stars. On these mini-planets, which are composed of densely packed atomic particles called neutrons, are small areas with gigantic magnetic fields firing extremely strong radio signals—and often light waves— into space. As they spin, they spray these waves across the face of our earth in cycles. Some pulsars sweep the earth every thirtieth of a second while others have cycles as long as 3.7 seconds.

CYCLES IN RADIO WEATHER

Before his recent retirement John H. Nelson held, for over two decades, the position of propagation analyst for RCA Communications. His responsibility was to forecast daily radio weather so that shortwave radio transmissions would not be interrupted by "poor radio weather."

Radio waves cannot travel in a circle around the earth. They must be bounced off the ionosphere, a layer of rarefied gas enveloping the earth 200 miles up. This ionosphere "ceiling" is created by radiation—particularly ultraviolet—from the sun. Whatever it is that affects radio communication is presumably something that affects the ionosphere.

We do not yet know what this "something" is, but Nelson discovered that it is associated with the angular relationship between the planets as viewed from the sun. Imagine yourself up in space looking down upon the solar system with the sun in the middle and the planets revolving at various distances around it. Draw imaginary lines from the sun to each of the planets. Each of these lines, of course, will be distant from each of the other lines by a certain number of degrees. If at any instant any three or more planets are so situated that the angular relationship between the lines connecting them and the sun is 15 degrees or some multiple of 15 degrees (Figure 61), the quality of radio propagation will be affected, provided one of the angles is 60 degrees, 90 degrees, 120 degrees, or 180 degrees.

Fig. 61: Planetary Relationships

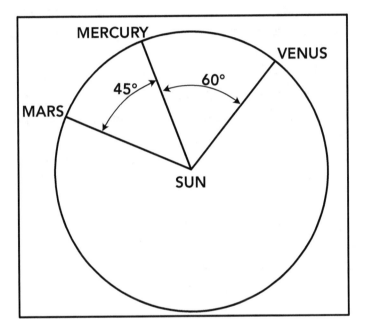

Diagram to show Mercury 60° (four times 15°) from Venus; Mars 45° (three times 15°) from Mercury and 105° from Venus. This configuration will affect the quality of radio weather.

For important disturbances there must also be at least two fast-moving planets and one or more slow-moving planets involved in the configuration. The fast-moving planets are Mercury, Venus, Earth, and Mars; the slow-moving planets are Jupiter, Saturn, Uranus, Neptune, and Pluto. The fastest moving planet is looked upon as the "trigger" planet. It is as simple as that—but it is still all very mysterious, and John Nelson is the first to admit that he does not know why certain angular relationships of our planets are associated with disturbed weather. But indubitably they are.

John Nelson's work has illustrated another successful application of forecasting based upon a knowledge of cycles. With this knowledge, according to the last report I had received, he had made 1,460 forecasts during 1967. His accuracy rating was 93.2 percent! His discovery that there is a correspondence in timing and time span between the cycles of shortwave radio disturbances and planetary cycles also shows how a knowledge of cycles can suggest the possibility of a cause that might otherwise be unsuspected. We must learn if there are correspondences between these planetary cycles of his and other phenomena here on earth. Are there corresponding cycles in weather, for example, or corresponding cycles in plants, or animals, or man?

Now you are perhaps aware of the scope of our mystery. Its clues are everywhere, from a tiny microscopic one-celled creature fluctuating in abundance in the waters of our world to quasars, pulsating in cyclic brilliance and energy over 6,000 million light-years away.

Is all this rhythmic behavior here on earth and "out there" merely coincidence? Let us gather together some of these "clues" and see what we have.

"The more extensive a man's knowledge of what has been done, the greater will be his power of knowing what to do."

—Benjamin Disraeli

13

The Ultimate Clue

E VERY SCRAP OF cycle evidence that we have been able to collect and preserve during the past thirty years can be found in our library at the Foundation. To the best of my knowledge our library contains the most comprehensive collection of cycle material in the world. It is divided into three main sections.

In the Data and Research section we have figures concerning several thousand "time series." A *series* is a string of figures arranged in some order. A *time series* is a string of figures arranged in order of time. "Average annual wheat prices in the United States since 1864" is a time series. So is "Average daily temperature at Boston since January 1, 1967." Here you can locate data about earthquakes, tree ring thicknesses, geological deposits, rainfall, temperature, barometric pressure, auroras, sunspots, planetary positions, wars, animal abundance, disease, prices, production, crops, transportation, trade, etc.

Many of the records go back for hundreds of years, some for a thousand. A few, such as war, sunspot maxima, geological deposits, certain tree ring measurements, auroras, and earthquakes, extend backward to the pre-Christian era. This section also contains the work papers from any research that we have done on any of these series of figures, either by longhand or by means of the computer.

The second section of the library is where we record the cycle work of others. It contains thousands of articles and clippings and books and reprints of papers in scientific journals alleging cycles of various lengths in the hundreds of phenomena in which such behavior has been observed.

If someone has written that there is a six-year cycle in the abundance of gumbos (or someone has written that there is *not*), you will find the information here if we have it. Each item in this section is cross-catalogued by branch of science. Thus if a particular paper alleges cycles of a particular length in weather, earthquakes, sunspots, and prices, it is cross-indexed under climatology, geology, astrophysics, and economics. Conversely, if you are interested in geologic cycles you could go to the geologic section of the cross-index file and find the names of all the papers we have in the library in which geologic cycles are recorded and alleged.

The third section of our library is perhaps the most interesting. It is concerned basically with interrelationships—and particularly with interrelationships that might throw light on the cause of cycles.

If someone discovers that snakes are more active when exposed to ultraviolet light, his paper about it is filed here. Then if it is ever discovered that the ultraviolet light reaching the earth has cycles of some particular wavelength, and that some biological phenomena have corresponding cycles, we may be able to get a hint as to the *mechanism* involved.

If radio weather fluctuates with planetary movements and angular relationships, as it does, maybe other behavior fluctuates this way also. We may not know just what mechanism relates the two phenomena, but we know that there is one. And the mechanism that serves to communicate to the earth the repercussions of whatever it is that happens when the planets bear certain angular relationships to each other may also be the mechanism that conveys faraway cyclic energy forces to earth. It is worth knowing more about.

I could go on and on about all the strange interrelationships that are alleged in the third section of our library. For instance, here we will learn that when pigeons are released in the neighborhood of radio towers, they cannot orient themselves; that if I stand near you, I will affect the flow of electric current from your hand to your head; and that artificial electric fields will cause dowsers' rods to dip. Some of these allegations need further corroboration, but they are all interesting and suggest that very minor electromagnetic forces may have very important physiological and psychological consequences.

Since a complete catalogue of cycles is as fundamental to cycle study as a list of animals is to the study of zoology, our library also contains thousands of index cards detailing specific cycles. As this collection grew, we were able to begin what has become a never-ending program of comparative cycle study.

Comparative cycle study is "the name of the game" so far as our work is concerned. We *compare* cycles in all phenomena, searching for similarities and possible relationships among them. For example, the fact that locusts have a seventeen-year cycle is, by itself, of little interest to us. But if apple crops also have a seventeen-year cycle we are intrigued. Is this mere coincidence, or is there something in the atmosphere that affects both locusts and apple trees? If so, what is it? And how does it operate?

If the cycle in one thing were unique and could not be related in length to the length in anything else, it would hold very little interest for us. The openings through which your hair grows change shape in cycles, thus creating wavy hair. But there is no reason even to imagine that a study of these cycles in several people would show any interrelationship. If there were, I would be interested. As there is not, I merely record this behavior as an interesting fact.

However, whenever we discover cycles that have the *same length in completely unrelated phenomena*, we are put on alert to the possibility that one of the behaviors is the cause of the other, or that both behaviors have a common cause. Of course, with the large numbers of cycles alleged in all sorts of phenomena it would be remarkable if there were not some with the same length merely by chance.

But if cycle lengths were random and completely unrelated, wouldn't you think we would have a fairly even number of cycles of each length, as many fifteen-year cycles as sixteen-year cycles, etc.? And if you discovered, instead, that cycles from completely unrelated phenomena seem to cluster around certain lengths while ignoring others, what would you think?

Consider, for example, the so-called 9.6-year cycle, of which thirty-seven out of many possible examples are listed below.

Is it conceivable that all these various behaviors could have cycles of the same length by chance alone? Or can there be some relationship among most of them?

THE SYNCHRONY OF CYCLES

Now we come to the heart of the matter.

During the past thirty years, as you have seen, we have discovered countless cycles that appeared to fluctuate with amazing regularity. Some of these cycles extend from before the time of Christ, and their rhythm has continued, almost without interruption, through wars, panics, revolutions, depressions, industrial change, and scientific advancement.

We discovered cycles that, after they were distorted, for unknown reasons resumed their old rhythm. We discovered cycles that continued to come true after their discovery. We discovered cycles with the same length and shape in many unrelated phenomena. We discovered that cycles seemed to reach their highs later and later as found nearer and nearer the equator. We discovered that cycles concentrate at particular lengths instead of being evenly distributed among all lengths.

Were all these pieces in our mosaic clues to the possible existence of cycles? Yes.

Were they proof that cycles exist? No. Maybe we were just playing games with numbers. Maybe it was all merely coincidence.

Then we began to look more closely at all the cycles with the same length, and what we discovered convinced not only me but a large body of previously doubting scientists that cycles are a reality.

The ultimate clue finally came to light!

We discovered that *all cycles of the same length tend to turn at the same time*! They act in synchrony.

Now if it is difficult to find cycles with identical lengths in unrelated phenomena by chance alone, think how much more difficult it is to find cycles with identical lengths that also *turn* at or about the same calendar time. What amazed us even more was to learn that *all* cycles of the same length behave this same way. The 5.91-year cycles all turned closely together, the 9.6-year cycles all turned closely together, etc. This was unusually powerful evidence that we were dealing with *real* and not random behavior.

Sit with me now in our reviewing stand and watch this evidence parade before your eyes in step to silent drums. But while you watch, you must not feel superior, for you too march to those same drums. You too are in the parade.

Cycles alleged to be 9.6 or 9.7 years in length in natural and social science phenomena

SCIENCE	PHENOMENON	PERIOD IN YEARS
Mammalogy	Colored Fox Abundance, Canada	9.7
	Coyote Abundance, Canada	9²⁄₃
	Cross Fox Abundance, Canada	9.7
	Fisher Abundance, Canada	9²⁄₃
	Lynx Abundance, Canada	9.6
	Marten Abundance, Canada	9²⁄₃
	Mink Abundance, Canada	9²⁄₃
	Muskrat Abundance, Canada	9.6
	Rabbit Abundance, North America	9.6
	Red Fox Abundance, Canada	9.7
	Silver Fox Abundance, Canada	9.7
	Skunk Abundance, Canada	9.7
	Timber Wolf Abundance, Canada	9.7
	Wildlife, Canada	9.6
Ichthyology	Salmon Catches, Canada	9.6
	Salmon Abundance, England	9.6
Ornithology	Goshawk Abundance, Canada	9.7
	Grouse Abundance, Canada	9.6
	Hawk Abundance, Canada	9.6
	Owl Abundance, Canada	9.6
	Partridge Abundance, Canada and U.S.A.	9.6
Entomology	Caterpillar (Tent) Abundance, New Jersey	9²⁄₃
	Chinch Bug Abundance, Illinois	9.6
	Tick Abundance, Canada	9.6
Dendrochronology	Tree Ring Widths, Arizona	9.6
Agronomy	Wheat Acreage, U.S.A.	9.6

SCIENCE	PHENOMENON	PERIOD IN YEARS
Climatology	Barometric Pressure, Paris	9.7
	Ozone Content of Atmosphere, London and Paris	9⅔
	Precipitation, Worldwide	9.6
	Storm Track Shifts, North America	9.6
	Magnetic Value	9.6
Hydrology	Runoff, Rihand and Sone Rivers, India	9⅔
Medicine	Disease Incidence (Human Heart), New England	9⅔
	Disease Incidence (Tularemia), Canada	9.6
Sociology	War (International Battles)	9.6
Economics	Cotton Prices, U.S.A.	9.65
	Financial Crises, Great Britain	9.6

THE MOST SIGNIFICANT EVIDENCE

What you are about to see needs little in the way of explanation. Here are five diagrams, each showing the timing of all available cycles of a particular length for which an ideal turning point has been calculated. The number of years in which each cycle has been observed is also included. *No cycles have been excluded because they didn't fall into our ideal pattern.* Furthermore, as new cycles are discovered, they almost invariably turn at the same established time of other cycles of similar length.

The dramatic concentration of the timings exhausts the possibility of mere coincidence. The demonstrated synchrony of behavior in *all* the phenomena that have been timed in each cycle length cannot reasonably be considered chance (see Figures 62–66).

If you study the five diagrams you will note that a few phenomena are inverted. These particular cycles have their lows while the others of the same length are having their highs, and vice versa. Thus we have a synchrony of turning points rather than a synchrony of highs and lows. It is the nature of some things to be upside-down relative to other things. When your outside temperature is high, the sale of fuel oil is low. When the yield of crops is high, the price of crops is low. When physical production is high, the number of business failures is low.

I suspended personal judgment in regard to cycles for many years. It was only after we discovered that cycles persisted over hundreds and even thousands of years, and after we were able to make comparative cycle studies that showed that substantially all the cycles of any given length turn at about the same time, that I became convinced without any lingering doubts as to the significance of at least some of these behaviors.

It is simply inconceivable that *all* the observed coincidences could come about as the result of random forces.

The mystery is real!

Fig. 62: The 5.91-Year Cycles on Parade

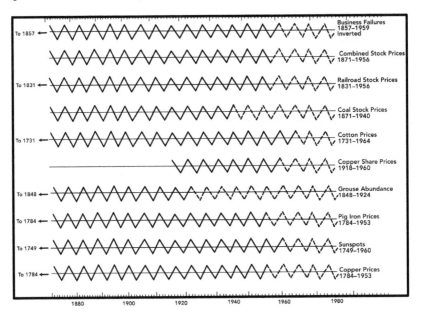

Diagram to show timing of idealized crests. Note that here and in the following charts crests come close to the same time. This fact suggests an interesting relationship.

Fig. 63: The 8-Year Cycles on Parade

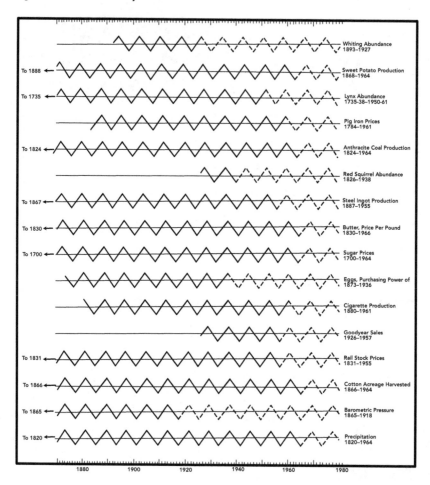

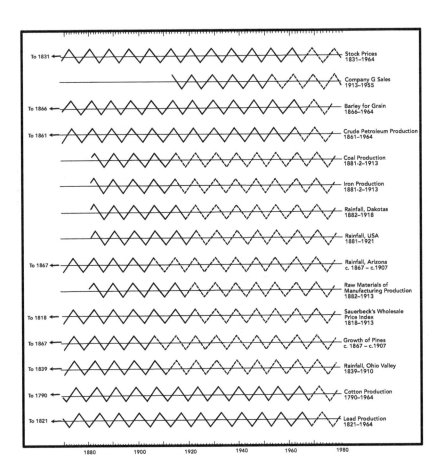

Fig. 64: The 9.2-Year Cycles on Parade

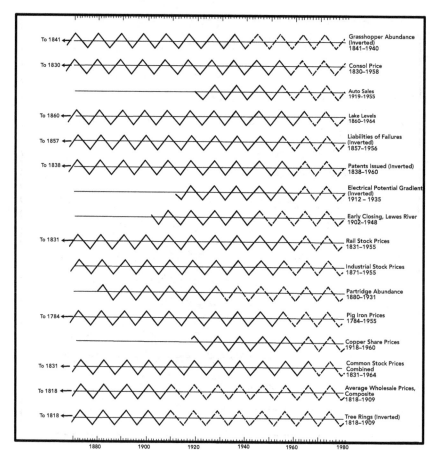

Fig. 65: The 9.6-Year Cycles on Parade

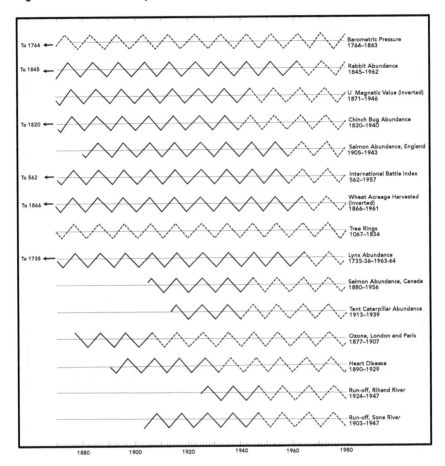

Fig. 66: The 18.2-Year Cycles on Parade

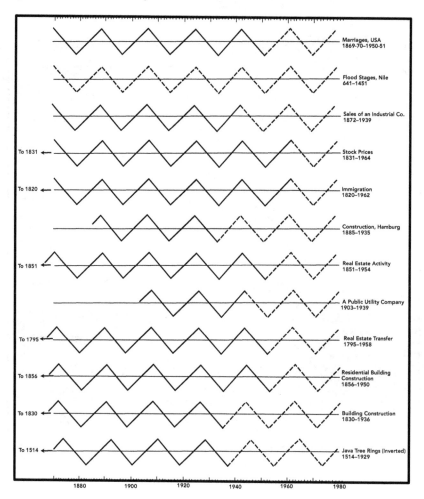

"Great discoveries and improvements invariably involve the cooperation of many minds. I may be given credit for having blazed the trail but when I look at the subsequent developments I feel the credit is due to others rather than to myself."

—Alexander Graham Bell

14

The Imperative Question

THE NAME TYCHO Brahe may be meaningless to you.

Tycho Brahe was a Danish astronomer who died in 1601, seven years before the telescope was invented. For over two decades he studied the moon and the planets from his island observatory near the Danish coast. At his death all Brahe's notes from his long years of lunar and planetary observations were left to an assistant, Johannes Kepler.

Before his death Brahe had developed a theory, namely, that the moon and sun orbited around our stationary earth while all other planets revolved around the sun.

Although Brahe was subsequently proven wrong, Johannes Kepler, using Brahe's voluminous notes and observations, finally evolved planetary laws of motion that were milestones in astronomy.

Later, flushed with emotion from his monumental discoveries, Kepler wrote, "Has not God himself waited six thousand years for someone to contemplate his work with understanding?"

With all deference to both great astronomers, and in great humility, the feeling has often swept over me that I am walking the same path traveled by Tycho Brahe... and I have already walked it ten years longer than he in my quest for an answer to *my* imperative question: "Are there unknown environmental forces, predictable in their effects, that influence human beings and other forms of life and even nonlife here on earth—and if so, what are they, and how do they operate?"

My quest has not been in vain.

I have noted, with great satisfaction and a tinge of pride, the tremendous upsurge in interest concerning the study of cycles in recent years. Since our Foundation became affiliated with the University of Pittsburgh several other universities have expressed a desire to establish Institutes or Centers of Comparative Cycle Research. A fresh air has blown through academic quarters, generated perhaps by our recent discoveries and adventures in space.

The increasing knowledge of cycles in human affairs has not yet provided us with complete knowledge of the future. Perhaps it never will, for even when we know all that is to be known of cycles, we will know only part of the picture. Consider man's elaborate study of the tides. Even with the known astronomical basis of tidal behavior computed to amazing accuracy, the most careful projections of the tidal forces are often upset by winds, which for the most part are utterly unpredictable for any great distance into the future.

Nevertheless, projections of cycle patterns do come true over longer periods of time and with greater reliability than forecasts by any other method known.

And so we persist with our imperative question, which in truth can be divided into three parts:

1. What is it "out there" that causes cycles?
2. How do these external rhythmic forces get transmitted to earth?
3. What is the mechanism whereby human beings, plants, and animals are affected?

We still do not know what it is "out there" that vibrates or cuts lines of force at all these various wavelengths, but science has taken great strides in the space age that supply us with at least partial answers to questions 2 and 3.

Now we know that the entire solar system operates in an electromagnetic field. Thus we know that things that happen "out there" *can and do* affect us here on earth.

But much more important from the viewpoint of cycle study is the accelerating accumulation of evidence that electromagnetic forces affect plant and animal life and even inorganic chemical reactions.

THE QUEST IS JOINED

A small group of brilliant scientists, working in different fields around the world, has contributed greatly in pioneering the inevitable solution to the great cycle mystery.

You will recall Yale's Professor Harold Burr's discovery that the electric potential of trees varied in cycles and that different trees varied in the same way even though separated by thirty miles. Obviously something external to the trees and yet common to them in both places was operating to cause this strange behavior.

And you will recall Northwestern's Professor Frank Brown, who discovered that the activity of both plants and animals fluctuates in cycles even when they are kept in hermetically sealed containers under constant conditions of light, temperature, humidity, and barometric pressure. A potato, kept under controlled conditions, evidences cycles and even predicts the weather two days in advance. More particularly, its metabolic rate goes up and down in a manner determined by some as yet unknown environmental force fluctuating with barometric pressure.

What causes these curious behaviors? Probably the potato growth is sensing geophysical forces that are also changing the weather. To discover what this force is, or what these forces are, Brown his conducted a multitude of experiments. In one experiment Brown let mud snails emerge from a funnel-shaped aluminum canal into an evenly illuminated arena. Their tendency to move right or left was measured on an underlying grid. The angle at which the snails crawled on the grid varied according to the time of day and the phase of the moon and could be altered by placing a magnet beneath the entrance of the funnel. Obviously at least some animals do perceive lunar variations in subtle environmental forces; one of these forces appears definitely to be magnetism.

In another experiment Brown found that the common planarian worm will turn away from a weak source of gamma radiation, and that these animals know the difference between north and south, east and west. (That's better than some human beings I know.)

Another contributor to our progress was Professor Y. Rocard, of the Sorbonne at Paris. Professor Rocard discovered that human beings responded to these electromagnetic forces too. He has followed dowsers (men with dowsing rods who go around looking for the best places to dig for water) with extremely sensitive instruments and learned that there are real differences in the magnetic fields in those places where the rods bent downward. Conversely, he has forced the rods to dip by exposing the dowsers to hidden artificial fields.

Even inorganic substances react to these environmental forces. More than 400,000 experiments, covering a ten-year period, by Professor Giorgio Piccardi, of Florence, Italy, show that the time required to complete various chemical reactions varies with the time of day, the time of year, the sunspot cycle, and whether or not the chemicals in his test tubes and flasks are protected from external electromagnetic forces by metallic shields.

What does all this add up to? Daylight!

No longer is it necessary for us to say "Things act as if *something somewhere somehow* acted on something that in turn somehow acted on us to make us act in a patterned way." We can now theorize that *something somewhere* acts on the electromagnetic field in which the earth is immersed and that this field affects the chemistry of our bodies to make us alternately optimistic or pessimistic, energetic or slothful, warlike or pacific.

We now have hundreds of well-authenticated cycles and thousands of allegations of other cycles to be restudied and reevaluated. Periods group at certain definite wavelengths. Things that have the same wavelength turn at about the same time. Cycles keep on coming true after discovery, and when distorted return to their former timing. Cycles go back continuously for hundreds and thousands of years; in fact, they have left their imprint on rock strata that are millions of years old.

A new science is taking form beneath our hands and eyes. New vistas invite exploration almost daily. Things are moving so fast and so favorably that it is difficult to keep pace with them. We are not "there" yet, but things have been pretty well roughhewn, and except for cause, *the discovery of which is merely a matter of time,* our mosaic is fairly well complete.

But much remains to be done and I have no desire to join Tycho Brahe until the great cycle mystery has been resolved. However, my desires count for little in the pattern of God and if it is not destined for me to carry this quest through to final victory it is my earnest prayer that somewhere there is another Kepler.

Perhaps it will be you.

Perhaps it will be you who someday will run his finger down a row of figures in a computation performed by Dewey in 1941, 1944, 1958, or 1970 and say, "Here. Here is the answer!"

The solution of our mystery is near at hand, requiring only much hard work—and time.

Time. I have lived with that word for the better part of my life. I have measured time. I have cut time into chunks. I have turned time back to explore pulsations long ago silenced. I have projected time into the future.

Still I cannot hold it back—and there is so much yet to be accomplished.

I am reminded of some words spoken by Dr. Reinhold Niebuhr at a commencement exercise several years ago:

> Nothing that is worth doing can be accomplished in your lifetime; therefore, you will have to be saved by hope. Nothing that is beautiful will make sense in the immediate instance; therefore, you must be saved by faith. Nothing that is worth doing can be done alone, but has to be done with others; therefore, you must be saved by love.